The Story of an Ordinary Woman:
The Extraordinary Life of
Florence Cushman Milner

*"Perhaps the most important autobiography of our era
would be the* The History of Nobody at All.*"*

Irwin Edman
Philosopher's Holiday

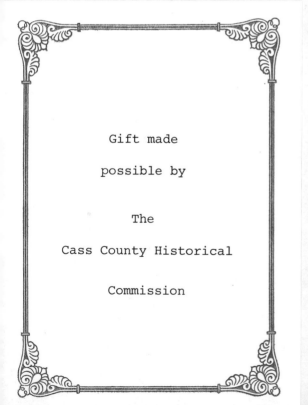

Gift made

possible by

The

Cass County Historical

Commission

The Story of an Ordinary Woman: The Extraordinary Life of Florence Cushman Milner

Edited by

Mary-Maud Oliver
and
Edward Surovell

Historical Society of Michigan
Ann Arbor, Michigan

ISBN: 0-9614344-3-0

Library of Congress Card Number: 89-85190

First Edition

Table of Contents

v

Introduction

As a title *"The Story of an Ordinary Woman"* is fitting because it is true. The story of a long life of activity recounts experiences, many of which are common to thousands of American women "all unknown to fame" and yet whose labors are responsible for much of the best in American character. Not enough credit has been given to one who performs every duty, humble though it may be, to the best of one's ability.

Florence Cushman Milner
Cambridge, Massachusetts

Thus begins Florence Milner's own story. It is a story introduced to me by her niece, Mary-Maud Oliver, some years ago. Indeed, Mrs. Milner's account of teaching in Niles, Michigan, a chapter in this book, appeared — somewhat condensed — in *Chronicle*, the magazine of the Historical Society of Michigan, in 1983. It was the only forum then available to the Society to let others know of her remarkable career. Now, the Society's Gillette Memorial Publishing Fund is available, so her whole story is published here.

Mrs. Oliver deserves much credit for this final product. Her careful watch over Mrs. Milner's personal papers and her diligent checking of references have made this autobiography a better product. Her patience as the manuscript was reviewed and edited is remarkable and very much appreciated.

Half-way through this effort, Mrs. Oliver sent along Mrs. Milner's personal papers. They brought to light aspects of her career not touched on in this book. Here she emphasizes her teaching, the students, her life and its changes in the late 19th and early 20th centuries. Consequently — and appropriately for a publication by the Historical Society of Michigan — it primarily covers her Michigan years. Her papers tell more of her life after 1916, after her move to Cambridge, Massachusetts.

Most noteworthy is the fact that Mrs. Milner wrote prodigiously. Among her books are *On Teaching Geometry*, 1900; *The Teacher*, 1913; editions of *Alice's Adventures in Wonderland*, 1912, *Through the Looking Glass*, 1914, and *The Rectory Umbrella and Misch-Masch*, 1929. She wrote articles for many magazines, including *The Bookman*, *American Motherhood*, *Detroit Saturday Night*, *The Boston Transcript*, *The Christian Science Monitor*, *The New York Evening Post*, *Yankee*, *The Schoolmaster*, *Michigan Tradesman*, *Education*, *Western Journal of Education*, *The Mother's Magazine*, *Forward*, *The Girls' Companion*, *Young People's Weekly*, *The Michigan Woman*, *The Modern Pricilla*, *Today's Housewife*, *Social Progress*, among others.

This is a list of which most writers would be proud. I suspect, however, that to Mrs. Milner it was just doing one's job to the best of one's ability.

Readers of our time may find Florence Cushman Milner a bit old fashioned; her style of writing is very much of the 19th century, to be sure. However, running through her comments about teaching are themes very much on peoples' minds today. She straddles two centuries. As Mrs. Oliver mentions in her comments, her lifetime experienced America's maturity as a nation, and her citizens — especially her women — broadened perspectives. To be sure, the trail blazed by Florence Milner — while perhaps minor in the larger picture of the women's movement — is a significant one, nonetheless. Together with others of her generation, she did lead the way for others who followed. It is good, therefore, that her niece persuaded her to put her life on paper.

This publication would not be possible without considerable editorial and preparatory efforts. Most especially, the careful review of the manuscript by Edward Surovell of Ann Arbor is appreciated. He caught many errors in reference and greatly improved the flow of the narrative. Donald M.D. Thurber, of Grosse Pointe, who fondly remembers Florence Milner from his own years at Harvard, provided some additional insights and recollections, as did Mrs. L.L. Vanderburg, of Dowagiac, and Walter Zabel, of Niles. Especially appreciated was Tod Oliver's careful review of the manuscript and editorial remarks.

Initial editorial review was provided by Nicolyn Steinhoff; text preparation was generously contributed by Roberta Ryan, Mary Ellen Wood, and Nancy Marshall. Composition and layout were by Bauer, Dunham and Barr, Ann Arbor.

Thomas L. Jones
Historical Society
of Michigan
Ann Arbor, Michigan

Preface

My Aunt Florence's autobiography reveals, I think, the development not of an "ordinary woman" at all; rather, she was very extraordinary, if in no other way than through the various posts she held in her 65-year career. Nevertheless, she chose the title and it reflects her own modest assessment of her career. You will think otherwise, I am sure. In this book she traces her life, from the perspective of 92 years, beginning with her childhood in Concord, New Hampshire, later school days in Dowagiac, Michigan, where at age sixteen, she began her forty-four years of teaching in Michigan, followed by twenty-one years in the Farnsworth Room of Widener Library, Harvard University.

My own personal memories of her are from visits she made to our home in Owosso and to the visits we made to her home in Detroit (in the Coronado Apartments at the corner of Seldon and Second Avenues). Aunt Florence had the great ability to enter into every situation with genuine interest and enthusiasm. On one of her visits to Owosso, my sister Adelaide's "Pow Wows" group was having a social on the spacious lawn of the Fred Gould home on West Oliver Street, to earn money for the new hospital to be built in the King Street woods. Florence thoroughly enjoyed the evening where tables were set under the trees from which hung Japanese lanterns, and ice cream and cake was served by the "Pow Wows," some in Indian costume. She later wrote an article about the event and it was published in a little magazine called *Every Other Sunday*.

My visits to her Detroit home are very vague, but she often

told me how much pleasure she and her husband, my Uncle
Sam, had in teaching me to sing and act out numerous nursery
games. She sent several hand-made books to me with beautiful
pictures and hand-printed poems and also a subscription for
several years to a delightful magazine, *Little Folks*.   In 1928,
Aunt Florence decided to visit every member of her family.
This trip took her to Chicago to visit one sister, Blanche
Cushman Murray, to Owosso to visit that sister's twin, my
mother, Maud Cushman Thompson, to Detroit to see a niece,
and, at the invitation of one of her former students at the
Detroit University School, Edsel Ford, to a reunion, a
memorable occasion. This trip also included a few days with
my husband and me and our children in Cleveland. All this
at age seventy-three.

We carried on a remarkable correspondence during the remaining years of her life. Upon re-reading her letters, I am impressed again with the wide range of her interests. She wrote
of books, authors, educational and political matters, her excitement over having seen John Guilgud in *Hamlet*, the Guten-
burg Bible donated to Harvard by the Wideners, and remembering attending a tribute to Ellen Terry in England and joining
the assembled actors and singers in the memorial performance.
She and her sister-in-law, Flora Milner Livingston, continued
their keen interest in Harvard athletics. When they could no
longer attend games, they listened by radio to every one and
sent enthusiastic reports to our younger son, who shared her
zeal, including score cards by which she kept account of every
player's record.

I had told her that I would be glad to take care of any or
all of her writings, and ten years after her death, they arrived
in many boxes. What a revelation was there: bulging notebooks
of her many interests; ten hard-cover notebooks of her trips
to Europe, including typed accounts of each day, plus programs
of performances attended, even hotel bills and menus, and clip-
pings and photographs.

She wrote her autobiography at my request, after retiring
from Harvard in 1937, at age eighty-two. I told her that I wanted
her life story for our children. In her later years, she often
thanked me for asking her to do something that had given her
so much pleasure. And now, the pleasure is mine and that of
my children, to share it with you.

As she was also involved in many writing projects, her hobby of "remembrancing" on paper continued until her ninety-second year. She devotes a number of chapters to her teaching years, in Dowagiac, Niles, Marshall, Grand Rapids, Ann Arbor, back to Grand Rapids, and finally as Associate Principal of the Detroit University School. Many of her students became important in the history of Michigan and the country. She was in close contact with many of them by mail and by personal visits when they were near Cambridge where she lived from 1916 until her death in 1950. On her 90th birthday she received over one hundred notes and ninety American Beauty roses from her "boys and girls" from the Grand Rapids days.

As one of her students at the Detroit University School was Edsel Ford, many persons had asked her what kind of boy he was. She describes here her contacts with him. In later years he had taken her for a walking tour of his regular rounds at the Ford factory. She wrote in one letter: "I was impressed by the fact that his relations with the heads of departments and the men, his familiarity with every process was the same as his schoolboy attitude — friendly, natural, modest, intelligent and efficient."

Her recollection of Edsel Ford naturally reminded her of her first experience in driving a "horse-less carriage" in Detroit in the late 1890's. While still living in Grand Rapids where she was preceptress of the high school, she made several trips to Detroit where her younger twin sisters lived. One was married to Willis Grant Murray, chief salesman for a large bicycle factory, and the other to George Edward Thompson, minister of the Second Presbyterian Church and my father. At that time, as far as she could determine, there were only three pleasure automobiles in Detroit. One was owned by Harold Du Charme and the other two were owned by the bicycle company where her brother-in-law was employed. He knew how interested she was in anything of a mechanical nature so he invited her to take a ride with him. She was delighted and gives a good discription of the vehicle and the experience of driving it herself on the return trip from out Woodward Avenue "as far almost as Palmer Park" and through the traffic to the Cadillac Hotel. She wondered if she might be the first woman to drive a car in Detroit.

Florence was born October 6, 1855, in Greensboro, Ver

mont. In 1857 the family moved to Concord, New Hampshire, where her father was employed by the Downing Carriage Company, which later became the famous Abbott-Downing Company. She vividly recalled her childhood, her Maine · mother and grandmother, her Vermont father and the school that gave her such excellent training from the time of her entry at age four and a half until she was ten. During her later years of teaching she was often asked where she had acquired her methods of instruction since she had had no formal training. Her answer was that as far as she could remember her methods were those used to explain problems when she was a child in Concord. She admitted that her methods wandered far from the rigid discipline of her two revered teachers but she emphasized logical procedure and meticulous attention to meanings, reason, good writing and spelling, as they had done.

Her family's home was across the street from the State House where there was a succession of exciting events during and after the Civil War. She recalled a meeting with General Sheridan when he was addressing a huge crowd from a platform in the Square. Florence also remembered being given a ride in the buggy of ex-President Pierce and that he always spoke to her in later days. One of her very distressing memories was on the occasion of "her" President Lincoln's death. She followed the symbolic funeral cortege to the cemetery, weeping copiously, but bewildered by the refusal of her father, whom she adored, to let her wear the mourning rosettes that all her little friends were wearing. It was many years later that she learned that her father belonged to the small group of "Copperhead" Democrats in New England.

In 1866 the family moved to Dowagiac, Michigan, where her father had obtained work. Her family and school and community life are recalled, especially the beginning of her love for writing. When she graduated from high school at age sixteen, she was immediately offered the position of teacher in the First Primary. Thus began her forty- four years of teaching in Michigan, all of which is recorded here. She also published two books, many articles, including a long series for the *Michigan Schoolmaster*, served on educational committees, and was in demand as a speaker for professional meetings. She was appointed by Michigan Governor Woodbridge Ferris as a delegate to the Women's International Peace Conference in St. Louis in 1915; she was the only Michigan woman so honored.

I found in one of her notebooks the following, written about her teaching experiences: "Only recently did it occur to me that through all my years of teaching I had never had a letter of recommendation, never applied for a position, never, except for one time in Grand Rapids, asked for an increase in salary, never took a teacher's examination, and never had a teacher's certificate until near the end of my service in Grand Rapids. At that time a state law was passed compelling all teachers to have a proper certificate. The School Board then made me a present of a Life Certificate. This is all true, of course, because my experiences began before the demands now made for something besides ability to teach and a pleasing personality, two qualities that are still most desirable if not imperative, in fact."

In 1916, my aunt was appointed head of the new Farnsworth Room in the Widener Library of Harvard University. She remained in this position for twenty-one years, with the added responsibility for the organization and direction of seven house libraries under the supervision of Robert V. Blake. During those years she continued to enjoy her contacts with students and faculty and to write numerous articles for publication as well as hundreds of letters, corresponding with former students and friends in Michigan and around the world.

Summers spent in England brought many opportunities for articles and pleasure. On her first trip she went with Flora Livingston, who was involved in editing the works of Rudyard Kipling. This brought them two invitations to tea at Bateman's, the Kipling home, a rare glimpse into the home life of this famous author. Florence's visit with Major C.H.W. Dodgson, the one responsible for the Lewis Carroll estate, made possible the permission she needed to publish her own editions of two of his books.

Florence retired in 1937 and until her last illness at age ninety-three continued to be vitally interested in all matters. As a young girl I stood in awe of her. Now, however, childhood awe has become abiding admiration. Her 65-year professional career spanned America's coming-of-age, from the Civil War to the mid-twentieth century. As such her life provides a very personal glimpse into this very complex era. From her view, she was "ordinary;" from our view, she was far from that rather modest assessment.

Mary-Maud Oliver
Urbana, Illinois

A Life Begins

I was born in the little town of Greensboro, Vermont, on October 6, 1855. The photograph that hangs above my desk shows a story-and-a- half house with roof sloping to the front just visible at the left and a sort of L addition made by later tenants. It is a typical New England cottage, painted white with green blinds. The little hill upon whose summit the house stands is slate green, with the emerald of the Vermont hills in the distance. Behind the house the hill drops suddenly to what was then known as Greensboro Pond. At the remote end of this hill-bordered, tree-fringed sheet of water has grown up in later years a popular summer resort. "Pond" did not accord with its modernity so it was rechristened "Caspian Lake," but to me it will always be Greensboro Pond.

When I was two and a half, in the year 1858, we moved to Concord, New Hampshire, into a little cottage across the street from the State House, the center of much excitement in those days of political oratory before, during, and after the Civil War.

My father was the sturdiest type of Vermonter, with backbone of New England granite, uncompromisingly honest, acting always with simplicity, and with no more consciousness of his virtues than are his Green Mountains of their beauty. By trade he was a wagon and carriage maker in the employment of the Downing Company, later merged with the Abbott Company. Since in those days work was mostly by hand, he could make his labor as honest as himself. I used to spend many childhood hours in the shop, where he taught me the names of the tools and the use of as many as my childhood hands could compass. Thanks to this early training, I can drive a nail straight and know the joy there is in the use of skillful fingers.

At one time it was my father's business to go into the country to buy stock for the large carriage factory. On these expeditions I was frequently his companion. They were driving trips, and he often handed me the lines while he looked at trees. He was a silent man, speaking only when he had something of importance to say. As we drove through the beautiful New England woods, he taught me the names of the trees and trained me to distinguish them by foliage, by bark, and by general contour. When we stopped at sawmills or lumber piles, he would point out the differences in the grains of wood until I knew oak, ash, maple, beech, and pine, whether sawed into boards or standing in the forest.

He trained my ear to the song of the woodthrush, the whistle of the quail, the notes of the bluejay, even its disagreeable caterwauling. Nothing in nature escaped his eye and his curiosity. Together we learned all we could of the world around us, but the greatest of the many silent lessons he taught me, simply being himself, was the lesson of absolute integrity to pledged word and to every obligation. Such integrity he kept constantly before me day by day in the fulfillment of every duty. I am sure he never preached. I do not remember that he ever talked about doing my duty. These principles were so much a part of him and so embedded in his character as to be taken for granted.

Vermonters are noted for their dry humor and my father was no exception. In one of our drives in search of lumber we passed through a little village, with its characteristic white church steeple surmounted by a brass rooster vane. "Florence," said he, "that rooster crows every time it hears another rooster crow." I don't know when I finally saw the joke, but I pondered over it for some time.

As to my mother, I wish I had the power to draw a picture which would honestly represent her. To begin with, she was beautiful, not only in physical features, but in every movement she made. How well I remember my rapture, as a small child, over her "dramatics" — the queenly lift of the head and her graceful movements as she swept into the room, skirts rustling, reciting a speech of Portia or of Lady Macbeth — sometimes with dishes in her hands as she set the table for our dinner.

My mother was possessed of high ideals and lofty ambitions.

William Washburn Cushman   **Mary Stimson Cushman**

Conditions bound her to a narrow circle, and its limitations often galled her high spirits. This made her doubly anxious to set my standards high and to open to me every opportunity that limited circumstances and a circumscribed life made possible.

From my earliest childhood she stimulated my love for reading and always had interesting material within my reach. She encouraged me to save my pennies and buy books that should be my very own. Pennies were scarce, but I well remember my first purchase — not a single book, but six volumes all at once. They were the "Lucy" books, written especially for girls by the author of the far-famed "Rollo" books. Rollo was in them, for he and Lucy were cousins. Jonas was there, too, and the model father and mother. Information in abundance was tucked in on every possible occasion, and no stinting in moral instruction, besides all sorts of hints on politeness for little girls. As literature, these books have shared with Rollo the ridicule of the present "authorities," but they held my interest much as Amy Lowell said the Rollo books held hers. I shall never forget the glory of their purple bindings radiant with gold lettering, nor the pride with which I looked upon the splendor that was mine and mine alone.

My mother, born in Houlton, Maine, was of French extraction, on her mother's side. From that strain comes whatever she possessed of joyousness and similar qualities that served to balance the somberness of the New England inheritance.

Our home was always simple, such as a mechanic in those days could give his family. The necessities were there; the adornments

— we called them luxuries — were always the result of my mother's eager reaching out for beauty, for the fulfillment of some of her higher ideals, or for a wider existence.

I knew later what deep longing for things outside her limited life seethed in her eager soul. Yet with it all she was joyous, making every opportunity yield its last drop of pleasure. Even now I can hear her merry laugh that rang through all my childish days.

Florence Cushman (standing), with her mother (center) and twin sisters, Maud (lower left) and Blanche

Early Education

When I was four and a half, my conscious, systematic education began. Ella, my constant playmate, had reached her educational majority and was to start school in the spring. The rules were stretched to allow me to enter with her. Since our little white cottage was just across the street from the State House and the school building was only across the Unitarian Church yard near by, my journey to and from school could be watched from my mother's room. There were no kindergartens then, so we were put at once into the first primary, but at that time no one seemed afraid that my nature would be warped or my intellect stunted by being set regular tasks.

I had already picked up, by what might now be called the natural method, a bit of education. On the hearth of the kitchen stove, the name of its maker and the place of its manufacture stood out in relief. By tagging my mother around and asking her over and over again what this or that letter was, I learned most of the alphabet. The name on the stove, I learned later, was "Tilden's Improved — Barre Vermont." Having mastered its fourteen different letters, the other twelve were mastered from a set of blocks. Next came spelling out words from a primer. According to modern methods, that was all wrong but my mother did not know that. I always pronounced "the" with full value to the long "e" and I read "I-see-the-cat" with a triumphant jump at the cat. In spite of these unscientific methods, I could read my primer fairly well before I started school.

I don't remember, that first day, about going to or entering school. I was just there, fascinated beyond words by what must

5

have been the droning of a primary school of the severe New England type, unrelieved by any of the schoolroom recreations common today, yet on that first day something caught and held me for life.

When the teacher caught me reading the words in the primer, she announced that on the morrow I could enter the first reader class. Between that day and this, there have been other successes, other triumphs, but none stands out more clearly. At dinner (dinner was at noon then) I announced after the first half day that when I grew up I was going to be a teacher. From that early decision there was no wavering until with full vested rights I stood before my first school of eighty-five small children.

The standards of this typical New England school of 1860 were rigid. It was not considered necessary to pay much attention to a child's whims or to consider school a place of entertainment. So there were no so-called nervous children demanding special treatment. If there were, they did not get it, and I suppose that there may have been casualties that were not known. We did everything on schedule. At the time set for arithmetic, we had arithmetic. Our moods were not consulted, and we never dreamed that the systematic and definite routine might warp our little souls, nor did our parents worry about the matter.

Arithmetic was very old-fashioned. We learned our multiplication tables by rote, recited them in a sing-song, and said the fives faster than the others. We had miles of mental arithmetic, where we had to repeat the example word for word after one reading by the teacher and then go through a prescribed reasoning process to the answer.

We had a spelling book and learned columns of words with puzzlers like "quay," "phthisis," "pneumonia," and "roquelaure," whose pronunciation gave little clue to the spelling. We did not know the meaning of half the words we spelled but when in after years we heard them, we did not have to go to the dictionary for the spelling. It was good training to stand in a row, toes hugging a chalk mark or a crack in the floor, watching with forward bending body those above, with mind alert for a missing vowel or a superfluous consonant that might offer a chance to "go up." "Leaving off head" is no great honor, yet at the time, it was very important and those trained in this "spell down" method made good spellers.

For reading, school boards did not furnish the supplementary readers or the treasure-full libraries of today. Each child owned his own reader and read it over and over again. The things in it were worth reading, too, as all McGuffy trained can testify, real storiesout of real literature, and frequent repetition left these masterpieces forever fixed in memory.

We had much practice in penmanship, with insistence that the penholder must point to the right ear. The teacher went about the room turning pens in the right direction, often saying, "What is that pen doing pointing over to Bow Crossing?"

As I look back, I am convinced that for that time — I might say for any time — this school in Concord was a good one. Here, until I was nine years old, I had only two teachers and these of the finest type of New England spinsters. I do not remember their names, but I do remember with gratitude the simple, honest direction they gave to my school days. They were as uncompromising as my father in matters of duty and demanded prompt and unquestioning obedience. They were sometimes stricter than modern methods would approve, yet in retrospect their severity is without condemnation. In two instances only does any feeling of injustice cling to my heart.

The teacher had directed us to sit with folded arms, "position one," I think she called it. I fully intended to obey, but my curls fell uncomfortably forward about neck and face. It was a stiflingly hot day. I unfolded my arms long enough to brush back the curls and returned immediately to the assigned position. I had disobeyed a definite command, and for such disobedience the uniform penalty was to bring the offender out in front of the school and administer six strokes of the ferule — I remember counting them determined not to flinch — on the open palm.

Yes, the punishment was over severe, but I had disobeyed a definite command and the teacher, without investigation, did not let "mercy season justice." My pride, as I remember, was not seriously wounded, for everyone was treated the same, conduct being interpreted strictly according to the letter of the law. Perhaps it was then and there that the lesson of unquestioning obedience to authority was driven home, for somewhere I did learn that lesson early. It may have saved me from serious calamity later. Who knows? The evils we escape unwittingly are never listed.

Another example of this stern discipline clings to memory. One day a little friend and I stayed after school to work out our arithmetic problems for the next day. She, being a thrifty little maiden, copied each example on her own slate as we went along. We were doing the work on my slate so each example was erased as soon as the answer was triumphantly reached. After we had finished, she left and I remained to get my own work ready. First I cleaned my slate with the bottle of colored water that we kept in our desks for that purpose. It took me some time to go over the work again and the lateness of the hour made me feel hurried. In my worry I could not remember one point in the last example. My friend's slate stood on the floor against her desk. I had done most of the work in the first place, so with no thought of cheating I looked at the slate by my little friend's desk. The teacher came slowly from the platform, took my slate, and in ruthless silence wiped it clean. She refused to hear any explanation. There could be none for cheating — such was the edict of her New England conscience.

Valuable and necessary as they are today, there was no law promulgated by the Board of Health and parents were not particularly anxious when their children were afflicted by such inevitable diseases as Chicken Pox and Mumps. No one thought of staying home if afflicted by mumps on one side only and no one had to be told by a doctor what the matter was — mother simply gave the victim a nice spoonful of vinegar and the diagnosis was spontaneous. I shall never forget the picture of that room. Boys and girls sat with swollen faces tied up in great handkerchiefs of various colors while frequent groans and grimaces testified to the suffering of the victims.

I have two other vivid memories of that school during my first year there — my first crime and my first love affair. During my early weeks at school the teacher made some changes in seats. The little girl who had occupied the one assigned to me had removed her reader, her slate with sponge tied to the frame, and her bottle of colored water. As I put my own small belongings into the desk, I discovered something wrapped in stiff white paper. I opened it and peepedcautiously. There was a beautiful pink gumdrop with crystals of sugar glittering on its surface while loose crumbs rattled in the paper. Automatically I popped the sweet morsel into my mouth. I did not set my teeth into it but, with New England thrift, allowed it to melt slowly in "linked sweetness long drawn out." When nothing was left but a succulent memory, the little girl came back for her pink gumdrop.

Had it been there I should have handed it over at once, but it was gone, gone forever, and its sweetness was fast turning to bitterness.

A child not yet five years old is not prepared to grapple with ethical questions. I saw no way out but the way of silence, to which I added the cunning of some criminals by entering into the useless search, for was not the sweet stickiness still on my tongue? The little girl cast one last look at the corners of the desk and went sadly away. To a little girl in the first primary even one gumdrop is a valuable asset. She doubtless forgot the loss very soon, but to this day, the sight of a gumdrop recalls the scene and brings back all the misery of the experience. In imagination and in my dreams I have bought tons of gumdrops to give that little girl, but I never could remember her name and I know not where in the wide world she disappeared.

The object of my juvenile affection was a little boy a few months older than I. He and the gumdrop girl and Ella are the only children of whom any impression remains from these first school years.

Charlie had beautiful yellow curls that fell to his shoulders in symmetrical ringlets, perhaps an image of Little Lord Fauntleroy. He wore a long-sleeved brown and white checked gingham apron, scanter than a girl's, and fastened with a shiny patent leather belt. We bestowed various infantile attentions upon each other. At all children's parties, he was my knight and if by any chance he seemed to prefer another even for a few minutes, my little heart knew all the torments furnished by the green-eyed monster.

One day word raced around the school that Charlie was to have a birthday party. His parents lived in a beautiful house, which seemed to me like a story-book palace compared to our tiny cottage. The fear of not being invited was almost too much to bear. My friends, whose mothers knew Charlie's mother, were sure they would be invited — but my mother did not know her and the girls said that Charlie's people were very rich and surely would only invite their own friends. I had never thought about riches before and still couldn't see how that could have anything to do with being invited to a party. Charlie and I were best friends and surely friends invited friends to a party — and I was fiercely loyal to my mother who was so young and so beautiful, in my eyes much more lovely than Charlie's mother. I had not yet learn-

ed that neither beauty nor wealth nor ability is the golden key
that unlocks the magic door to society.

However, this story turned out in my favor for the precious invitation did come and the relief was great. Saturday came at last.
I can remember distinctly the dress I wore — white ruffled with
a broad pink sash with shoulder knots of pink fluttering against
my neck and arms. There were the several stiffly starched skirts
underneath and shiny shoes. The house was a castle that day —
the long parlors had been transformed into a garden of beautiful
flowers and I walked about in a dream. The party was to begin
with a march in which each boy was to take a partner, with
Charlie leading. My heart stopped when I heard Charlie's mother
call out, "Come Charlie, take Edith and stand in the doorway until we get the others in line." I was actually trembling — Charlie
to choose Edith when he and I were Valentines — I wanted to
run away, but just then Charlie asserted himself and the velvet
suit and yellow curls marched over to me as he announced to
his mother "I am marching with Florence." How proudly we led
the march, hand in hand, in and out the gaily decorated rooms
to the dining room where refreshments were to be served.

There is no sequel to the story. He went his way and I went
mine but the experience, never forgotten, taught me that children
are more than children and that all their thoughts are not of dolls,
toy trains, and tin soldiers. The emotions may be fleeting, but
they are serious and important while they last and call for sympathy and understanding.

My father's puritanical upbringing was responsible for my learning to play cards when very young. "I don't propose to have
a child of mine sneaking off behind my back to learn to play,"
said he, so he began lessons long before I could reach the table
from an ordinary chair. Many were the pleasant evenings thus
spent in close companionship with my parents. Dancing was also
part of my early education. With but the three of us in the family (the twins had not yet arrived), my first instruction in the old-
fashioned contra dances was accomplished with a chair for the
fourth. Thus, I learned forward and back, ladies change, balance
to the corners, dos-a-dos, with my father cutting all sorts of
serious and comical capers with his chair partner. My mother
taught me the waltz, not the stationary one of modern times but
the slow and graceful one of that period.

Because there was no one to stay with me whenever my

parents went out for an evening, it was necessary for them to take me along. My father made a little sleigh for me, with high back and sides, all well upholstered. When I was rolled in a blanket and nested in it, even the New England cold could not touch me. Thus, I went everywhere my parents went. One evening someone came for them in a horse and cutter. In my sleigh I trailed along behind, my father holding the rope over the back seat. It was an exciting ride, for the bumpy road and the speed of the horse was quite unlike the slow pace on the sidewalk. The jingle of the harness, the light, rhythmic hoof beats, the swift sailing over an endless expanse of white snow made me feel that our destination could only be Heaven itself. *Our* destination, however, was a friend's home in the country where a supper and dance were being held. I was allowed to go through a quadrille or two with my father before the sandman claimed me. Then I was comfortably bestowed, as were the babies in Owen Wister's *The Virginian*, to sleep away the hours, but not, so far as I know, to be traded for a more or less desirable child.

The principle business of the Downing Company, which was founded in Concord in 1816, was the building of coaches, which ran overland before the days of the railroad. The Concord Coach was well known on the coaching roads of New England and the far west, and even as far away as Africa. Some were built to carry heavy loads over the difficult roads, seating from six to twelve passengers. Others were elegant, ordered by special design by hotel owners. Potter Palmer of Chicago had selected a number in a bright yellow for his establishment. Many others were ordered to individual specifications as to color and upholstery, type of ornamentation, and scenery to be painted on the doors.

At the time of my father's employment, the storehouse of the Downing Company was a fairyland of make believe to my little friend Ella and me. There before our eyes were rows and rows of these coaches ready for distribution, but for us, charming playhouses. They were an especial delight to Ella, who was such a dainty child with a flair for imaginative games, and even I was quite willing to follow her lead and play "lady" in them. We named the aisles for Concord streets, selected our own dwellings, and located well-known families in others. Naturally we took the handsomest coaches for ourselves. If there was an especially elaborate one on the floor, forehanded Ella claimed it before I could tear my mind away from playing the game. If the gorgeous

The Concord Coach (c. 1852)

one I saw recently displayed in the Concord Station was in the storehouse in those far-off days, Ella lived in it. We made ladylike calls, leaving our cards according to the mode of the day. Together we knocked on the door of Mrs. Corning, Mrs. Eastman, and Mrs. White, and asked at the desk of the hotel for some senator or famous general we had heard our mothers say was stopping there. We held a mirror up to nature as we reproduced the manners and conversations of our elders.

Another vivid childhood experience persists. My mother had taken me one day to Haverhill, Massachusetts, to visit my aunt. Late on the afternoon of our arrival, there was suddenly great excitement around the house and my mother and my aunt rushed off to Lawrence, leaving me slightly bewildered in this strange environment. When they returned, much later, there was more excitement in their voices and manners — and a bag of candy for me. The talk of the elders was all about a mill, with the name "Pemberton" rumbling heavily at intervals. The flavor of the candy was new and not especially pleasing then, although later it became a favorite. The word "Pemberton" and the strange flavor thrust forward in memory — real mysteries until they both cleared to bitter almond and the tragic fate of Pemberton Mill. At that time, January 10, 1860, this was one of the country's major disasters. Nearly seven hundred men, women, and children were at work when, without apparent warning, the building trembled, tottered and fell, killing at least one hundred and in-juring many others. To me, the exponent of the calamity is still bitter almond, the latter always flashing the disaster to mind.

Although my father rejected the oppressive austerity of his childhood, there was complete loyalty and devotion to our lit-tle Universalist Church. Attendance was taken for granted as was the Sunday morning ritual of baked beans and brown bread. No one ever asked, "Are you going to Church?" or "Who is going to Church?" When the last bell began to toll we would be on our way. We always sat in the second row in one of the wing pews on the right side of the church. One Sunday my parents walked down the long aisle with me just behind them. When my mother took her seat half-facing the congregation, she noticed that many of her friends were smiling. Later she learned that I had gone down the aisle bowing low to all the family friends, thus putting to practical use my lessons in politeness.

After the arrival of my twin sisters and as soon as they were able to attend church with us, we always marched in, in the same order. My mother sat in the further corner of the pew with my sister Blanche at her side. I came next, in the middle, with Maud at my left and father on the outside. I often used to wonder what would happen had there been any more in the family. That we could sit anywhere else or in any other order was outside con-sideration. Sunday school was equally a matter of course and everyone but my father attended. He used to go home and start dinner. How very sacred to me is this early training. My world was dependable.

In later years I have not always gone to church or Sunday school, but I am more than grateful that in my childhood the question of church or not church was never up for discussion. No matter how far one may wander from those conventions, the value of such early training in them cannot be overestimated and eventually it triumphs.

I suppose the following embarrassing experience is familiar to most adults brought up in a church-centered life. What were called Sunday school concerts were held in our Universalist Church once a month. The program consisted of recitations and music. I must have been about six when selected to "speak a piece" at one of them. My mother drilled me carefully, and on the appointed night I walked confidently to the platform and began

Be firm whatever tempts thy soul
To loiter ere it reach its goal
Whatever siren voice would draw
Thy heart from duty and its law, Be firm . . .

And there I stopped, unable to think of the next line. To get a good running start, I began again but could not get over the hurdle. In spite of my mother's gesticulations and the minister's suggestion that I take my seat, I began a third time. Then the minister returned me by gentle force to my mother while all the way my voice rang out, "Be firm."

Between the schoolyard and the grounds of the Unitarian Church, instead of a gate, there were posts. These were the days of crinoline in its most expansive stage. The posts were far enough apart to allow me and my hoopskirt to pass easily, but I had watched ladies with their skirts billowing out behind as they crowded through the narrow space. To produce a similar effect, I used to snuggle close to one post, hold my skirts close to the other side, and watch with pride the balloon effect that seemed as fine as that produced by ladies.

The next experience was not so happy. Surrounding the school grounds was a fence of square-cut rails anchored at intervals to stone posts: the same sort of fence that once surrounded Harvard Yard. The rails were so placed that the sharp angle was on top, offering a chance for skillful walking almost as good as a tight rope. At this time I must have been nearly five years old.

I negotiated the rail successfully, even climbing over the intervening posts. When I reached the corner I stepped on the flat tip of the post and jumped. Alas, I did not reach the ground. My hoopskirt caught on the post and held me dangling there for I know not how long as I frantically tried to disentangle myself. Fortunately the principal of the school happened along and unhooked me.

General Sheridan and President Pierce

All the parades, processions, civic and state functions centered in the State House grounds across the street from our home, so my life during the Civil War was literally spent in the midst of troops and troop movements. I have vivid memories of these years, and yet they seem to run together into a huge panorama of continuous activity with only a few definite events standing out. Striking among these was the military funeral of a soldier — and there were many during this period. Always there was the somber dirge played by the band or by the fife and drum corps as it led the doleful march to the cemetery. There was always a long procession of carriages, and the horses stepped handsomely in seeming dignity and respect. All was slow and somber on the way to the cemetery, but on the return, the rollicking tune played by the same band or fife corps left my mind in confusion.

War scenes, almost inevitably the same, come to mind. Days and nights seem filled with troops going or returning by way of the State House, where speeches were made, bands played, and carriages of friends or relatives of the soldiers gathered, bringing gifts of food and love for their departing men or shouting in joy at their safe return. Railroads brought crowds to the city, flags waved everywhere, bonfires lit the sky at night, and the State House yard was filled with tents.

I vividly remember my fright one day when I returned home, dashed into the hall and found a sick soldier asleep in the hall bedroom, and being cared for by my mother.

But that was almost trivial compared to the terror that seized me when on several occasions I returned to find my father, normally a quiet, reflective man, engaged in a violent dispute with his best friend. My father was a Copperhead Democrat and his best friend was an equally staunch Republican. Their fierce arguments almost lead to physical blows as they shook their fists at each other, to prove the rightness of their convictions. That my father should have been such a violent Copperhead, even a supposedly peace-loving one, has always been a mystery to me. He was born in Vermont of the sturdiest Pilgrim stock and had lived in that state most of his life and had never been out of New England, but he was definitely in that group intensely loyal to President Pierce, even in the days of his "fall from grace," and was utterly opposed to the Civil War.

Most intensely vivid is the memory of my grief when my father would not allow me to wear a mourning rosette at the time of President Lincoln's death, as all children were allowed to do regardless of politics.

I found some solace later for the sacrifice of the rosette. Like many other cities across the nation, Concord honored her President by observing funeral rites in the State House yard, with all the proper pomp and circumstance. I remember only the long funeral procession following the gun carriage, draped with the flag as though the form of the great man rested there. To me, he was there and not one of my rosette-wearing friends wept as I did. Blinded by tears, I saw little of the long military procession followed by a mourning citizenry which I joined, but the slow dirge of the drums beat its mournful message into my very soul.

It must have been then that the seeds of Republicanism were sowed into my mind to sprout later into a dogmatism almost equal to my father's, only on the other side.

As the war drew to a close, the excitement of the marching soldiers, the blue of the fresh uniforms, the sound of the fife and drum, and the gorgeous colors of the floating flags gave way to the return of the shattered armies and the sight of the "breaking ranks" of those companies of the Granite State over in the State House yard. I missed the excitement, but occasionally some great hero passed through the city and again my childish heart was glad at the crowds and the tumult.

One bright, sunny morning my mother sent me downtown on an errand. I wore a brown and white checked long-sleeved tire with the inevitable, torturous, straw shaker on my head. My mother, as always, started me from home with the strings tied demurely under my chin in a proper bow. A block from the house, the bow had vanished and the shaker was hanging down my back with the strings tied in a hard knot, the only way to wear a shaker with any comfort.

Thus emancipated, I went on my way rejoicing. I was just as happy and unconcerned when I met one of my playmates arrayed in her Sunday best, a dainty blue dress, a flower-garden hat, white stockings, patent leather ankle ties, and with her hair in shining braids down her back.

Courtesy: New Hampshire Historical Society

New Hampshire State House (c. 1860's)

I had done my errand and had added to my personal appearance a brown paper parcel (carrying brown paper parcels was not considered proper in those far-off days), and to the tangle in my hair by the frequent dragging on and as frequent dragging off of the offending shaker. No worry of this sort, however, entered my mind as my friend called out to me, "Hurry, hurry to the State House. General Sheridan is there and everybody is going to see him." I was delighted and gladly rushed off with her in perfect unconsciousness of my everyday attire as contrasted with the holiday dress of my companion.

We joined the stream of people and I soon found myself at the foot of the platform, with my shaker pushed back out of my way and my hand still grasping my brown paper parcel. I knew nothing — I saw nothing but the great and famous man before me. I wondered how such a famous general could condescend to speak to this throng of people who had never fought a battle or done anything the least bit heroic.

"This is a little friend of mine, General. She may be glad some day to know she once shook hands with you." The familiar voice attracted my attention and I looked up to see the governor of the state, who was a good friend of my father's. At last it dawned upon me that he meant me, and just as I opened my eyes in amazement, I was lifted to their level, shaker, paper parcel and all, and the great general was stooping to kiss my cheek.

When I was put down from the platform, my feet scarcely touched the earth as I flew across the street to tell the stupendous news. I burst into the house, nearly breathless, and shouted out my exciting story before anyone could interrupt. It seemed to me I had never been so happy or so near the clouds floating on high.

"And you went to see General Sheridan in that calico apron and shaker and carrying a paper parcel in your hand?" exclaimed my shocked and humiliated grandmother. "But, Grandmother, my apron was clean," I protested. But even as I spoke some sense of the enormity of my offense against the conventions of dress burst upon me. I realized that I had erred, although I could not see clearly just how. For the first time in my life I learned that the world held a "philosophy of clothes" that my child mind had never grasped.

The new knowledge brought a heavy cloud to a radiant day and the cloud has never quite lifted. I feel more and more convinced that my childish standard of an apron that should be clean and whole and the child happily unconscious of her clothes, was a much higher one than the modern overconcern and attention often spent on "what the young child should wear."

I was eight years old when the twins arrived. They were so tiny that they seemed like the smallest of dolls. I remember how my parents carried them around, each on a tiny sofa cushion. My father took the responsibility for Maud whenever he was home and my mother for Blanche. They were identical and it was impossible for anyone outside the family to tell them apart. My grandmother became quite a steady part of our home at this time because of the death of my grandfather. She played a very important part in our lives. As a small child, I held her in awe and almost fear. She was a typically austere New Englander, sharp- tongued, and critical of me and my ways.

One last memory of Concord remains. What is now a thickly populated part of Concord was once a beautiful wood surrounded by a fine stone wall, the property of President Pierce, who at the time of which I write had returned to private life.

These woods were rich in trailing arbutus, the mayflower of that region. We children used to go there for flowers too — freely gathered, but I distinctly remember treading on leaves with an awesome consciousness of the privilege. It seemed as though I was approaching very near to the presidential presence by being allowed to wander in the woods of the great man.

One day as Ella and I were leaving the woods with hands filled with flowers, a gentleman drove up from behind us and asked us if we would not let him drive us to the city. I knew at once that the speaker was ex-President Pierce. He must have loved and understood children, for in spite of our silence he reached out an encouraging hand and helped us into the buggy. I shall never forget the reverence that filled my mind as I sat by his side. I don't remember anything he said to me; in fact I'm not sure that he spoke at all. I was conscious only of a great exhilaration and exultation at being so honored. When he set me down at the corner of my street, I reached up and gave him my flowers. He took them with a kindly smile and I have felt that the flowers paid silently the homage of my spirit.

Out West to Michigan

W hen I was about ten years old, in the year 1866, my father was offered an opportunity to work at his trade in what, to a New Englander at that time, was "way out west." Accepting the offer, he moved his family to the little town of Dowagiac, in southern Michigan.

Our new home was a tiny cottage, set well back from the street, in a grove of young oak trees, but tall enough to make our front yard a green canopied marquee. A porch ran along the front of the house. From this, a central door opened abruptly into a tiny so-called parlor. To the left was a small room intended for a parlor bedroom. Back of the parlor was the dining room, with my mother and father's room opening out of it. Back of all was the kitchen and, New England fashion, a woodshed attached. From the parlor the steepest of stairs climbed to the chambers under the sloping roof, for the house was a story-and-a-half cottage. My twin sisters occupied one of the tiny rooms and the other was my castle.

The little room opening from the parlor played a small part in early training. Instead of using it as a guest room, my mother rather ambitiously called it the library, although the supply of books was limited to the corner whatnot and small table. My set of *Lucy* books was there on one of the shorter shelves near the top, the purple and gold still untarnished. Of some of the other volumes I have a fairly fixed picture although I never read very far into any of them. There was somebody's *Life of Louis Kossuth* with a flag of gilt on the back, *The Planter's Victim*, a Civil War story bound in red, and *Dred: A Tale of the Great Dismal*

21

Swamp. My childish reading of the title was *Dread the Tale of the Dismal Swamp*, and I used to wonder why anyone wanted to read a story he was commanded to dread. I did read most of *The Life of the Empress Josephine* and the pictures drawn of her native home have remained with me. Best of all was my mother's autograph album, a square book bound in red leather. It contained sentimental steel engravings and much poetry, some quoted and some original, written in the precise slanting penmanship of her young days. On the table was the large Bible, resplendent with gilt tooling and clasp. My father had purchased it at an auction and brought it home one day, rather apologetically, because my mother never quite approved of his weakness for auction sales. But I'm sure it was a good one, for it has survived, clasp and all, even unto this day, with births and marriages faithfully recorded.

The Cushman Home in Dowagiac

Calling this room a library gave to the books a definite place in a home and a forward-looking attitude toward reading, another instance of my mother's constant struggle toward her ideals. No doubt she had visions of a book-lined room which was never to be hers, but as with everything else, she stood on tip-toe and reached as high as she could.

Calling this room a library gave to the books a definite place in a home and a forward-looking attitude toward reading, another instance of my mother's constant struggle toward her ideals. No doubt she had visions of a book-lined room which was never to be hers, but as with everything else, she stood on tip-toe and reached as high as she could.

Later, through the strictest economy, a piano was acquired. It crowded itself into this little room, which thereafter was called the music room. The whatnot and the Bible went into the parlor.

My mother loved music. She had a very fine voice and had high musical ambitions for me. She sacrificed greatly to give me piano lessons, but I proved a disappointment. Silence often proclaimed that practice was not going according to schedule, and my mother, upon investigating usually found me curled up with a book, sometimes under the piano where I had once or twice eluded her eye. Although I got as far as playing "The Storm," "Falling Leaves," and "The Maiden's Prayer," my interest clearly did not lie in that direction so I was set free and the opportunity was passed along to the twins, who at a very early age were practicing eagerly and later played in many concerts throughout the area.

In this little house my mother met her first real responsibility for the total care of the family and of the house. My grandmother had assumed much of the work in the East so my mother and I learned together. I cannot think of any phase of housework that we did not master, though tears of discouragement (and perhaps dislike) were often in her eyes as mistakes were made. There were none of the helpful appliances considered indispensible today. There was not even an ice box. An occasional chunk of ice was purchased and wrapped in a piece of carpet and kept in the cellar in a tub. We learned to cook on an old black wood stove with a good arm to take the place of the electric mixer, to sweep with pieces of wet paper scattered to keep down the dust, and to clean without any miracle products. We learned how to churn with a dasher and were rewarded by such buttermilk as I can only dream of now. We learned how to make soft soap in a big kettle over a fire in the back yard, with lye and grease conserved carefully. This was a long and tedious process. Since there was danger of burning the soap at the sides of the huge receptacle, much vigorous stirring was necessary. The boiling was sometimes violent and frothy, and although a common occupation in many homes it did involve some danger, as I learned one day when my dress caught fire. Quick action on the part of my mother saved me from serious damage. Dishwashing was made endurable for me through the learning of poetry pinned over the kitchen sink.

All these experiences were of great value and were the basis later for sympathy with my girl students, who came to school from homes where the entire work of the home devolved upon mother and daughter. I have often been glad that I knew how to do these chores.

Much of the family life during the long summer days was lived on the porch and under the trees. All the work that could be carried out of doors was done there, and the supper table, whenever weather permitted, was spread under the sheltering oaks. The memory of these suppers and the close companionship afforded us as a family make me very grateful. For, in spite of the heavier work involved — a fact that eluded me at the time — my parents were so selfless in their loving and their living that no extra work was considered important if we had happy times together.

Back of the house was an acre of ground. This was my father's garden, which he cultivated with me close at his heels. I learned to plant cucumbers, corn, and all common vegetables. I learned the characteristic way in which each sprouted, grew, flowered, and came to full fruition. I learned to peer into the heart of apple blossoms and tell whether they bore promise of fruit or would only flaunt a wealth of bloom. My father taught me to thump a watermelon and tell whether it went "punk," to watch the color of corn silk and know when the ears were ready for use. We set poles for climbing beans and brush for peas. We watched in early spring for the first wrinkled leaves of rhubarb, later for ripening strawberries, and we fought potato bugs constantly and valiantly. All this I learned without knowing that I was doing anything but spending happy days with my father. The harvest of this companionship was a keenness of vision, an interest in all beautiful details of inanimate life, alertness in discovering new ones, and a sensitiveness to their beauty although my father never prated of beauty.

Limited means made it necessary for my mother to do most of her own sewing in addition to the housework, and I realized much later how very difficult it was for her. A new dress was an event to be come by only through the strictest economy and much labor, for dresses in those days were feats of engineering, not the simple nothings of today. The dainty organdie, flower-sprigged, that she was working on one day was nearly finished. It was made over a heavy waist lining to assure the firm, close fit then in fashion. The seams were boned and carefully overcast, all by hand, of course. At the last, the lining was to be cut low, leaving only the sheer material over the shoulders. In doing this, however, the scissors not only bit through the lining but through the organdie also. The waist, with its many bonings and much featherstitching of seams and overcasting, was a wreck. For an instant, my mother looked aghast, but she did not give way to any outward lament. I can see her now, almost at the instant, reach for new material and begin to cut out a new waist. I was but a child at the time, but throughout my life, when faced by discouragement, that picture comes to mind to give me courage.

Another picture of my mother's spirit when faced with a distasteful task is recalled. For a time, we kept a cow. My mother had had no experience with animals and loathed everything that had to do with the care of them. When my father, who did the milking, was taken ill, there was no one to perform this necessary task, so as always my mother rose to the occasion. The cow was tied to the fence and I was stationed at her head to see that nothing happened to the knot. It was a hot summer night and flies were a torment. My twin sisters, little as they were, were put on the other side of the fence to take turns at holding the cow's tail through the bars to keep her from switching it in my mother's face. My mother took the stool and attacked the milking. To some it may be a comical picture, and I will admit that at this distance my sisters and I are able to laugh about it, but we did no laughing then. That badly tethered cow, the pinioned tail, three children all afraid of the poor beast, and our mother equally so, but with her head resting on the cow's flank while tears streamed down her face as she tried to do her best at a supremely disagreeable task, did represent tragedy then. In spite of tears and terror, the job was done somehow, and none of us, including the cow, was the worse for the experience.

After we had been in Michigan for some time, my grandmother finally decided to take the risk of venturing into this wild west country to pay us a visit. My parents had tried to persuade her to move west with us, but nothing could induce her to live "the primitive life on the frontier." She was persuaded that Indians still threatened and that the requirements of a respectable life were as yet unattainable. To her west was west and the fact that Dowagiac was a town of two thousand or three thousand inhabitants, on the direct line of the Michigan Central Railroad from Detroit to Chicago, had no power to change her mental picture. The idea must have still persisted in spite of my mother's reassuring letters, because when she finally did arrive she brought a kerosene lamp supposing that we were having to use candles. When she saw our tiny but comfortable house, she looked about in surprise and remarked, "Why, Eliza, you do look real comfortable."

During the long perspective of years, this grandmother stands out in strong relief. As a child, I had no affection for her. She possessed none of the usual grandmotherly traits, was sharply critical of my actions, and often was an obstructionist who stood between me and some childish heart's desire. After that first visit to Dowagiac, she was with us for long periods, but not permanently until advancing years made it necessary for her to have a settled home.

She said that she was born "way down in the state o' Maine, in a small town near the Aroostook line." In reality she was born in Woodstock, New Brunswick, in 1806, at a time when the early settlers thought that they were within the borders of United States, and she persisted in that belief. She was proud of her state and the strength of character and conscience that was a part of her heritage. From her own "Maine" mother, however, was added a stream of French blood that gave sparkle and vivacity to every one of her words and actions. This was probably why she never became a "sit-by-fire" type of grandmother, but went alertly and efficiently about her household tasks to the very last day of her eighty-five years.

She belonged to an age when caps were in vogue, but she wore hers with a difference. They were of black lace with nodding flowers or bows of bright silk ribbon. I never remember seeing her with the then fashionable black silk apron for afternoon. No aprons for her except for housework. She probably wore spectacles but her brilliant dark eyes sparkled through them in a way to eclipse any glasses. She was also very fond of any dress that she could wear "to mill or meetin'."

On moral questions she knew no compromise, and if I am not a pattern of rectitude it is no fault of hers. She never failed of the sharp goad of some terse saying to drive me in the way I should go. There are a few scars left even today from the wounds of her well aimed shafts pointed with proverbs. They always someway hit the mark and did good service in trying to keep me on the straight and narrow path.

During years of residence in Michigan, my frequent quoting of my grandmother's sayings brought amused appreciation because of their unwestern flavor. On returning later to make my home in New England, I found many of these familiar expressions still in use although no one else seems to have been so persistently brought up on them as I was or to remember one to fit almost every occasion. I find it impossible to call them up at will, disassociated from a proper application. Lately I have been catching them on the wing as they appear for apt use. Many came directly from "Poor Richard." If things did not go exactly as planned her invariable answer was, "No use crying over spilt milk" or "Part of the loaf is better than no loaf at all." If, as so often happened, I wanted something beyond the limited means of the family, she helped me meet the situation with the good advice, "Cut your coat according to your cloth."

If I ever had anything approaching vanity, this grandmother plucked it out by the roots. She tolerated no pride in looks or clothes. To the "nothing to wear" excuse, she was ready with "Fine feathers don't make fine birds" or "If you behave as well as you look," which she evidently doubted, "you'll do." Her scorn of the overadorned, especially if she suspected the finery was beyond the means of the wearer, expressed itself with "Dressed to death and drawers all empty."

We all know the delight of loitering over pleasant occupations especially when one is called to less attractive duty. Out of such malingering, I was often roused by "Lazy folks take the most pains," a remark that still nettles in retrospect. There was not a lazy bone in my body, but when something pleasant came my way unexpectedly she rarely failed to say, "The lame and lazy are always provided for." When the opposite of laziness sent me plunging headlong into activity, the brakes were applied with "The more haste, the less speed," or "Make haste slowly." When I reached the age to receive the attention of young men, she, with early marriage a standard, chided me for my indifference to what she considered a good prospect, with "You'll go through the woods and pick up a crooked stick at the last." But I didn't.

That "Procrastination is the thief of Time" was thoroughly drilled into me, and it is the only bit of her philosophy that I have felt like repudiating, for I was overtrained in that direction. Punctuality has been the thief of my time. With the fixed habit of never being late, I am usually ahead of time for appointments and have waited untold hours for the unpunctual. It is well to be warned that "Time and tide wait for no man," but the lesson can be too thoroughly taught.

I was not the only target. Fawning ways, overelaborate clothes, and affected manners in anyone were but scant covering for foibles and flaws and she usually had a sharp saying upon which to impale all such failings. Her favorite comment on anyone of whom she did not approve was, "You can't tell by the look of a frog how far he will jump" or "It's hard for an empty sack to stand upright" or "The steam that blows the whistle never turns a wheel." When integrity was in doubt, she'd say, "I wouldn't trust him as far as I can throw a meetin' house by the steeple." Her supreme disgust at any lack of honesty was expressed by, "He'll say anything but his prayers."

She was equally sharp at pointing her shafts against herself. In our family, there was never any discussion on Sunday morning concerning church. It was taken for granted that everyone would go and at the proper moment the entire family would emerge from the front door — in Dowagiac, it was the same as in the East — of the Universalist Church. One morning my grandmother announced that she was not going to church, but arguments of the family finally prevailed and she went with us. Because the twins were too young either to go or to be left behind, evening attendance was not the habit, but on this particular night grandmother insisted on going. With a twinkle in her eye she remarked, "I'm like the pig. They had to pull his head off to get him into the trough and his tail off to get him away."

In Winter, after the dishes were cleared away, the dining room was the family rallying place. The lamp was placed in the middle of the table and beckoned to many quiet evenings. As my sisters grew older, they were allowed to stay up for a longer and longer time and to bring their little games and occupations to one side of the table. They were "doll" girls with a strong leaning to paper dolls. The replenishing and enlargement of the wardrobes of these dolls were, as I remember it, their favorite amusement. The few samples remaining show quite an ingenuity in the designing of costumes, according to the latest fashion plates, apparently. Heads of ladies and gentlemen were cut from some magazine and mounted on heavy paper and then suits and dresses of various colors and styles were cut to fit, with draperies and trains and sashes of different hues carefully pasted on, some elaborately decorated with a gold trim and huge puffed sleeves made by shirring thin pieces of paper and binding with a plain band. Each doll was named and many were the adventures of these paper doll families. I can remember distinct amusement at their pleasures — I suppose from my lofty eight year superiority and my complete lack of any interest in such occupations. Now, for the first time, as I gaze at the remains of their activity, I can see the imagination and creativity involved.

One Winter I became intensely interested in reading about Arctic explorations. Even now, any suggestions of expeditions to the frigid zones, a newspaper article or casual remark, transports me not at first to the poles but to this little lamp-lit room, warm and cozy from the glowing fire in the airtight stove, and the two windows that looked out over snow-piled sills to the unbroken expanses of the white sleeping garden. The lamplight falls on the beaufiful face of my mother with head bent over some task that would add to the comfort or joy of one of us. It falls on my father's sterner face, his eyes fixed upon his book, upon my sisters who were so alike that no only outside the family pretended to tell them apart.

My father would get up occasionally to feed the fire. If the opened door revealed a find bed of coals, he reported the fact laconically. He was a man of few words. The remark was enough to send my sisters for the corn popper, corn and butter. There was always a trip to the cellar for apples which my father pared, quartered and divided equally.

I cannot leave the story of this little cottage without a word about my tiny room under the slanting roof and pleasures therein. When we had company or on very cold nights in the winter, the parlor fire was lighted. In my room was a big drum, a round or oval sheet iron affair through which the stove pipe coming up through the floor from below allows the last bit of heat to be utilized before the smoke goes into the chimney. On fireless nights, we children scudded through the cold parlor to the equally cold rooms, made short work of undressing and plunged deep into a bed with a temperature only slightly modi fied by a hot flatiron or brick wrapped in flannel.

Evenings when the room was warm, it became my sanctuary. It was my joy to draw the little table close to the drum and there revel in a new book just discovered in the school library or dream over a sheet of paper, pencil in hand. Here, just for the delight in the doing, were produced stories, poetry, sketches, and what were called "essays." This fascination for writing has persisted, and a sheet of virgin paper always stirs the longing to write something on it, but it has not produced anything vitally important in the writing line. Once there had been the comfort of thinking that if the need of earning my living had not been so imperative I might have accomplished something valuable with my pen. Although I have written a good deal and have published modestly, long since came the conviction that my ability was little above average or no obstacle could have stopped me, for "Genius finds its own road and carries its own lamp." Always, however, just back of my main interest which became that of teaching, has lurked the love for writing with irregular indulgence in salvaged scraps of time.

In this little room, a journal was kept into which went my most secret emotions. I spent my hard-garnered savings for a case that locked. The journal was written, more or less regularly, until I was twenty-four years old.

On reading it over at that time, it struck me as being morbid or sentimental. As my intention was to be neither and it did not seem an honest or truthful record of the girl I really was, I burned it. I have never regretted destroying it although I have occasionally wished I could peep between its covers. In later years I made attempts at keeping a diary but these all went the way of the first. The last holocaust was a package of "Line O' Day" books covering fifteen years. After all, the record of a life is the resultant individual.

The things I wrote were secretly cherished but evidently I had not taken sufficient care of my papers, for one day the twins discovered them. At a safe distance they began reading aloud from them to my utter dismay. I made a dash for the papers but the young torments ran out of the house and led me a merry chase through grove and garden. They also proved that "He that runs may read," for they shouted the lines back to me and actually learned one stanza for future use. They have long since forgotten the lines but they were burned into my memory:

"Up in the morning early Before the birds begin to sing
And see what bright, rich treasures They will always to
you bring."

The world did not lose a great poet when I turned to teaching.

It must have been about this time that some of us conceived
the idea of writing a school paper. Anything that had to do with
writing caught my attention at once, and I went into the project
with energy as most of the work devolved on me. The little
magazine was much like others of its class, containing stories,
poems, locals, and jokes when we could think of any, and an occasional illustration. It was written in double columned pages
on foolscap, in imitation of a paper called *The Little Corporal*,
which was popular at the time. We named ours *The Little Captain*. To my knowledge no copy survives. If one existed, it would
make a sorry showing by the side of Lewis Carroll's "The Rectory Umbrella" and "Misch-masch."

There were many attempts to earn a few pennies by various
means, but the outstanding example of a budding businessman
was our popcorn boy, who built up quite a business for himself
and later sold newspapers in Grand Rapids, taught himself law,
and became a United State Senator, William Alden Smith.

As for school work itself, at the time of my high school years,
the course was very simple. Graduation did not mean any such
education as falls to the lot of the high school student today,
although many of us were inspired to know the joy of reading
good books. I do not remember that we had separate courses
although some took Latin and some did not. The Latin was poor
and there was little of it. We read one book of Caesar and three
orations of Cicero. To this was added a little algebra (very little),
plane geometry, fairly good work in English, general history, and
one term of German. At some point both ancient and modern
languages were deleted from the course, much to the indigna-
tion of some of the parents.

The week before commencement was devoted to public examinations, and these ordeals were attended by townspeople,
students, and alumni. It sounds very cruel now to contemplate,
but as I look back, I believe we simply accepted this final examination period as part of the expected routine of life. For any
student to fail in such a public manner would have been a
catastrophe.

There were only three in my graduating class, and on that day

I was offered a contract to teach the lowest grade in the Dowagiac schools beginning the following term, for $320 for the year, to me a princely sum. So at the age of sixteen I was started on a teaching career that was to last for forty-four years in the state of Michigan.

Dowagiac and Niles:
A Teacher at Sixteen

My own fitness for the position of primary teacher was only a training in faithfulness to duty, which the home rather than the schools had given, and boundless enthusiasm.

Nothing but the courage of youth and the audacity of inexperience could have made me venture into that room with eighty-four little children, half of whom had never been in school before. But some guardian angel must have hovered over me throughout the year, for at its close the school board, instead of turning me out, promoted me to the higher class in the next room.

By the spring of my second year of teaching, I had saved enough money for a few months of school. I was poor but I was ambitious, and I was hungry for an education. I had heard of a small school that was very cheap, supported by the Universalist Church, and not very far away, so in April 1874 I ventured to Smithson College in Logansport, Indiana.

The five months at Smithson were the happiest that I could have imagined. There I indulged my fondness for books and my yearning to know. Under the shade of a huge tree in front of our one building, I first found Thackeray and Trollope and they have never ceased to satisfy. The teachers were good teachers and devoted to their profession. Their books were always available to their students. One white-haired man stands out prominently in my mind. He lived alone with his books and his musical instruments. These treasures had crowded the owner from room to room until his whole house, save one room with its great four-poster bed, was surrendered to them. Young people and children loved him and to all who cared to come, the house was freely open.

Here I spent many long and happy hours, reading from his library and listening to his wonderful talk about his books, which he knew as one knows friends, wandering from room to room where the precious volumes crowded and jostled each other for shelf space.

After classes were over for the day, two special companions and I made our pilgrimage to the forest adjoining the college grounds. The path led along a high ridge that wound in and out among the great trees, twisted and burned and broken by a tornado of a few years before. The path led to the edge of a bluff for a glimpse over the valley. Sometimes, we would plunge down the steep side just for the sake of the tumbling and the rugged pull up again.

Some afternoons, if there was time, we would go on until we reached the old canal with its unused locks, then on to a glen hidden by the hills, down which a stream tumbled. In the early days of spring we would return to the dormitory laden with sprays of dogwood, pink clusters of redbud, violets and mayflowers. In autumn there was the regal glory of scarlet sumac, with its stiff plumes of deeper red, the purple ironweed, brilliant goldenrod, and later the scarlet berries of the haw and the wahoo, with crimson trailing vines and feathery clematis.

The college was coeducational and thus promulgated various rules for keeping youths and maidens apart. These were but a challenge to the enterprising to invent ways of breaking them, and so the society of very ordinary young men became exceedingly desirable in the face of opposition. But on one Saturday in June the rigid discipline was lifted and we were allowed to have a picnic together. Of course it was properly chaperoned, but fun was found in spite of this. I can remember how my particular swain of that day and I hurried on ahead down the ravine out of sight of the teachers, but for no reason except to be beyond them. We wandered back again in the twilight with the others, swinging the luncheon basket between us. I can even remember the sense of good comradeship that thrilled from hand to hand across the handle of the basket, but unfortunately the name of the young man who held the other side of the handle

Smithson College (1871-1878); as Michaels Business College, the structure was destroyed by fire in 1896.

is beyond recall.

The only flaw in these delightful months was the realization that they must end soon, for my father was not well and I was near the limit of my finances. One November day brought a telegram offering me the position of teacher of algebra at the Niles High School, in Michigan, a few miles from my family in Dowagiac. I was to leave immediately, for I was to be allowed only one day to visit the school, and was to start teaching on the following morning. There was relief in the knowledge of the offer, but heartbreak at leaving Smithson.

I sent a telegram of acceptance and hurried to the woods for a final armful of flowers, I arranged them in a big red jar in my room — how I loved this tower room of mine on the third floor. The view from my window had been my special delight and I sought refuge for a long last look.

I arrived in Niles late the next afternoon, and went to the accepted boarding house known in all small cities in those days. Here I had a little sitting room and a tiny bedroom opening from it. I had only time to make myself tidy before going down to supper.

Although I was no older than my friends in college, I had always seemed older and was always at ease with the older people I had known up to this time. Now, for the first time in my life, I was struck with a strangeness — painful shyness and timidity. I looked around the table and noticed immediately that I was dressed very differently. Most of the other women were young and married. There was a certain dash about their apparel, but I couldn't quite see what was the matter with mine. I had always made my own clothes and had never before been conscious that they were not all right.

When I returned to my room I studied myself in the mirror and discovered that the stock was too big and too deep. I took out my scissors, narrowed it, drew it closer and fastened it with a fancy pin as I had noticed one of the young ladies had done. I had just completed this repair when a knock at my door announced that Mr. Thomas, the superintendent of schools, was downstairs to see me.

How I wished that I did not have to appear before him. I had the crushing realization of how badly I looked and my heart beat furiously as I entered the parlor. He was kindly and courteous, but his black eyes told me how disappointed he was in what he saw. I could only answer his questions in monosyllables and I knew — how clearly I knew — that he was certain that he had made a mistake in hiring me, although he said, "If you can carry the work through successfully, we will pay you the regular salary in January." I was sure that he was convinced that I could never do it and that he must begin to look for a replacement.

I could hardly control myself until I reached my room where I threw myself on the couch and wept. I was lonely, discouraged, terrified. I am very sure, however, that, in spite of my fright, it never occurred to me that I could fail. I was determined to prove Mr. Thomas wrong and to succeed as a teacher.

Monday morning I set off early for the school where I was to visit my classes throughout the day. I entered the main room with Mr. Thomas and was faced by 150 boys and girls. All eyes were intent upon me and these were not boys and girls as I remembered my high school friends. These seemed like men and women, and many were as old or older than I.

Class followed class, and although difficult I did feel that with much work I could handle them, until the senior algebra class. One group of four boys came in together, every one was six feet tall and all at least eighteen, as was I. As they passed, one of them gave me a look of real sympathy, which helped mightily. That class left me weak and panic-stricken. My only preparation for this subject had been in Robinson's *Elementary Algebra* when I was fifteen years old. This class was using *Olney's*, a hard text, and the class had progressed far. If my life had depended upon it, I could not have done those examples, and the very next day I was to be in charge.

I went to the bookstore, bought the algebra book, and locked myself into my room. I started at the first page and worked through the problems, page by page. Some of them had a familiar sound, which encouraged me somewhat, but hour after hour I plodded on. The midnight bell sounded but it was two o'clock before I had caught up with the class assignment.

The first day went off much better than I had expected. It seemed as though the students were really trying to impress their new teacher, and if I hadn't been so aware of Mr. Thomas' distrust of my fitness for the position I would have felt half-contented.

Succeeding days went much as the first. I studied every night harder than I had ever thought possible. There was the rude awakening one day of the need to take a stronger hold of the class. I had assumed that they were eager for learning, but alas, what a mistake. It took all the ingenuity that I could summon to make sure that each student completed the work and that I kept them interested.

Algebra was still my chief battle, and by hard study I managed to keep two weeks ahead of the class. But finally I struck a snag and could not solve a certain set of problems. Over and over again I followed, or thought I did, the directions in the text, but I arrived each evening at the same dismal failure.

The day of the lesson I went to school early in fear and trembling. The weather didn't do much to help my spirits. The wind was blowing with its early December penetration, the air was filled with whirling snowflakes, hard and pelletlike.

I reached my room and concentrated again on the baffling problem. I had looked up the formula a hundred times and it seemed to be just a matter of substitution but something was wrong. All but the eleventh set came out right. I went round and round in that same rut that led nowhere.

The day passed with the other classes going on as usual, but finally the gong struck for my fatal algebra class. Emotions crowded upon me. I thought of condemned criminals approaching their hour of execution and was sure that I knew something of their feelings. I thought of the awfulness of disgrace before this class. I even wondered what was the earliest train I could take for home and how I could manage to pack the large black hat with trailing plumes that I had just purchased with my first month's pay.

The students began to gather and those seniors looked formidable that day as I thought of the disgrace ahead of me. I watched closely as they came in. George, Edward, and John were arguing about the problem, on a point that I recognized as my own stumbling block. Anna flounced into her seat with a disgruntled remark to Jennie, "I can't do a single example. Can you?"

I couldn't hear the answer, but Jennie's gurgling laugh indicated that whether she could or not, she wasn't going to let it trouble her greatly.

Frank Russel sauntered in with his usual self-possession, stopping at the window to watch two squirrels frolicking in the great oak tree outside. I wondered if he had been able to solve it. It was a real struggle to find my voice, my breath came hard, blood rushed to my head, and I could hardly see. I felt sure that all must be able to hear my heart beat. I sent them to the board and watched breathlessly to see what they could do. Anna had written her name and then taken her seat. Jennie was starting out exactly as I had done, so I knew that nothing but failure awaited her. I knew every turn of the wrong way. George and John were arguing again.

Over in the corner, Frank was working away with his accustomed calmness. I saw in a minute that he was not attacking the problem as I had done. I walked over to Frank and trying to keep the eagerness out of my voice asked, "Why have you set aside that two-tenths?" As I queried him further on his method I could see it all. I simply had failed to notice that in this set of problems the decimal had changed as well as the rule of progression. I went back to my desk and quickly re-worked all eleven problems. How utterly stupid I had been. But now the light dawned. Thanks to Frank, I taught the class as one inspired. My long and almost hopeless struggle made me appreciate the difficulties with a personal sympathy that would have been impossible otherwise. Never again could I feel impatience at the struggle of students, for I had suffered mightily. It all came about so naturally that Frank never dreamed that he had saved his young teacher from open disgrace. From that time on, Frank became a little apart from the others, a little nearer than the rest.

In later years Frank and I became fast friends. I confessed to his having saved me from disgrace and asked if he had wondered at my questioning him so closely.

"No," he answered, "I just thought you were the sharpest teacher I had ever known. Your questions were so to the point."

Indeed they were. The situation was desperate and I knew exactly what I needed to know.

Miss McClellan: A Model for Life

I was most fortunate in having Miss McClellan for the precep-tress of our school. She was an unusual woman. I knew when I first met her that she was different from anyone I had ever known before. The contrast between her gracious speech and my commonplaces, between her ease and my awkwardness, between her knowledge of the courteous conventions of life and my ig-norance of them made me determined to improve myself. For the first time in my life I realized that there is a difference bet-ween really walking and simply getting from place to place. She walked with ease and grace and set an example for me in every field. She gave a new standard for manners and led to new ideas in many directions. She was a mature woman. Born and educated in the south she had brought into the northern schoolroom something of the grace of her native environment. She was possessed of unusual personal charm and was a leader in all the societal functions of the little town.

She moved about the assembly room at school as though it were a drawing room and these young people her guests. The room itself reflected her personality, for she had been many years in charge of it. There was a large open space in front, with the platform at one side and the recitation seats facing it. The seats for the pupils studying in the room stretched in long rows across the rest of the room. On the walls were well-selected pictures and busts, and occasional full-figure casts upon bookcases and brackets. Blossoming plants were in such places as could be given up to them without interfering with the light and comfort of the students. Three columns had thrifty growing vines twined about them. All this gave a harmonious setting for Miss McClellan and one in which she moved as though it were her home. Above all, she possessed a personality that enabled her to control this room full of boys and girls without apparent exertion.

She was kindness itself to me. In my unsophistication she must have sensed my earnestness. My recitation room opened out of the assembly room and the preceptress became my daily study. Each day I felt I was gaining in influence and ability, but I was also very conscious of my shortcomings. Each day brought a stronger love of teaching and a conviction that someday I might become a good teacher.

My life was uneventful this fall term. Days were absorbed in teaching and evenings in study. I attended church each Sunday and knew a few people by sight, but the life of the town was completely unknown. I had been too eternally occupied with my own struggle to pay any heed to local affairs.

One night, however, I received an invitation to a reception to be given by the mother of one of my boys. She lived in one of the finest houses in town. My first feeling was one of delight, quickly followed by dread. I had nothing to wear that seemed appropriate. I had never attended a reception and all kinds of questions made my mind heavy. What time should I go? Should I arrive at the exact time indicated or should I plan to be a bit later? These are burning questions to one not used to social customs. It is only when one is a part of such life that it makes no difference.

I agonized over the matter for a day or two and then went to Miss McClellan with my difficulties. "I don't know," I added in conclusion, "that I have anything suitable to wear. I find since I came here that my few clothes are nearly all wrong in some particular." She rose to my need and offered to come to my room to look over my dresses to see which would be most suitable.

I took out my best black dress for her inspection, but Miss McClellan said that it was too old looking. To my green one she thought that it would do very well, softened a bit at the neck line, and that my black hat and gloves would be right with it, but she asked whether I had a lighter gown. I showed her my white wool dress that I had felt was not proper so had left it in the bottom of my trunk. This appealed to her immediately so she asked me to try it on. She looked admiringly at it and asked, "How did you ever find a dress made so simply and yet perfect in every line?"

"I saw a photo of a Reynolds portrait. I liked the dress and copied it. I make all of my own clothes with the occasional help of a sewing woman," was my answer.

"Well, this is the perfect dress for you to wear. Now try on the big black hat." This was the hat with the long black plumes that I had bought with my first salary.

"There. See how it sets off the dress. Now with long black gloves, you need not give your clothes a second thought."

When the eventful day arrived, I dreaded the ordeal and wondered how many mistakes I might make. Miss McClellan's one piece of advice had been, "Just keep your eyes open and when in doubt as to the conventional response, do the natural and kindly thing. With that rule in mind you'll never be in consciously bad form." I looked at myself critically in the glass and felt assured that my clothes were all right. I reminded myself of my grandmother's maxim, "If you act as well as you look, you will pass."

Courtesy: City of Niles Historical Museum

Niles High School (c. 1870's)

As I approached the door, it was swung open by a maid who directed me upstairs. The hallway and the room were impressive and the stairway wide and curved. As I ascended, trembling with dread and excitement, I held my head high to prove that I was not. Mrs. Tuthill, the hostess came to greet me. She was so very cordial and graciously assured me that there were many mothers there anxious to meet the new teacher. "If all the young people talk about you as much as my George does, we all ought to know a great deal about you by now." This was a shocking but rather pleasing bit of information. I had had no idea that the boys and girls gave any thought to me out of school. The same comment greeted me as I met the other women, and I was delighted.

Once I stood alone for a few minutes, floated into the corner like a bit of social driftwood. Surrounded by strangers I stood intently watching the company. The scene was new to me. I had never been in so large and so handsome a house. The great rooms, crowded as they were, imparted a sense of space that I loved. What a walk it would be from one end of the room to the other if empty. The flowers lifting their fragrant heads from various jars and vases excited me. The soft rugs and the beautiful furniture, the well-dressed women and the fragments of conversation that floated to me — the merry repartee was entirely new to me and I liked it. I rejoiced in it and longed to be a part of it.

Miss McClellan sought me out to take me to the dining room. There was a big bowl of red carnations in the center of the table. The glow of the candles through the scarlet shades, the pretty china, the delicate ices and fancy cakes all touched a part of my nature before unawakened. Several of my girls were assisting in the room. How different they looked in this light and with what real pleasure they came over to greet me. They talked freely of things of local and personal interest, and I found myself chatting with them as freely as though they belonged to the "crowd" at college. They accepted me as a human being and just as young in spirit. They didn't know that I was also as young as they in years. How I much I learned about my students — how Frank had always lived in the country until this year and how he hated the city, and was always running off to the woods and bringing back "stuff that nobody knows about." He was definitely the donor of the bittersweet and frequent sprays of wild flowers I found often on my desk. I learned that Ed was a great orator and hoped to become a senator someday. And so the conversation went with the mothers introducing themselves in between snatches of information and all too soon it was time to leave.

The clear December air thrilled me with the physical joy of being alive and how happy I was. I had been in the school for two months and although I had been close to failure, I did now feel that I was gaining ground and that in time I would succeed. The afternoon had widened my horizon and my heart was dancing with joy.

The Christmas vacation was at hand and also the time of my

testing — the end of my probation. The whole week was given over to examinations and I did dread it. I knew that I was being tested rather than my pupils. Mr. Thomas had visited my classes frequently, made suggestions, and once or twice had criticisms to make, as had Miss McClellan. They had seemed friendly but how anxiously I awaited their decision.

The examinations were all held in the assembly room. Each term Mr. Thomas made out the questions for three or four of the subjects and this term senior algebra was one of the ones he chose. It would be a severe ordeal for me. When I saw the questions I felt encouraged. I felt that my class should do well. I watched them anxiously. They seemed to be equal to their task.

The long awaited but dreaded summons to see Mr. Thomas came and I went to his desk. He greeted me with a smile and the blessed words: "The board has directed me to say that in January your salary will be the same as your predecessor."

"Then I haven't failed?" My eyes were filled with tears of relief.

"No, I'm free to confess that when I first saw you, I anticipated failure and we did begin to look for a replacement. You were much younger than I had expected and much younger in experience than in years, even. I've found, too, that you were more at home in a schoolroom than in receiving gentlemen callers." We both smiled in remembrance of that first "awful" meeting.

With this beginning and with Miss McClellan for a model, I walked home on air. The last day, with my desk laden with Christmas gifts from my students, I thought no one anywhere could be happier than I and I looked forward to the next term.

As school closed, Miss McClellan appeared and to my utter distress told me that she was leaving the school to be married. Completely selfish and forlorn, I wailed, "But what can I do without you? I have depended on you for everything." She told me that no one else knew yet except Mr. Thompson and the board. They had all seriously discussed putting me in charge in her place but decided that I was too young to be burdened with more responsibility, but that the time would soon come, if I continued to improve as I had so far.

There are a few other memories of community affairs. One experience will always remain vivid. My early religious training had been in the Universalist Church. There was no such congregation in Niles; the people I knew best were Presbyterian, so naturally I attended that church. Dear old Dr. Eddy, the minister, was like a patriarch of old, with his long white beard and shock of white hair. The spirit of Christianity was the wellspring of his being. Under his teaching I lost sight of problems of creed and learned about religion pure and undefiled. I made up my mind to join the church without troubling about the Thirty-nine Articles.

It was during this time that the great Temperance Tidal Wave and the Praying Crusades were rolling across the country and Niles was swept into the turmoil. The four orthodox churches of Niles united in a great revival service. It was all new to me and I attended the meetings diligently, seeing in it a great drama, but remaining untouched emotionally. Everyone became hysterical and there was a united effort to bring in a tremendous harvest of souls. The young high school teacher became a special target. She was deluged with letters from people of all ages and classes. Even the superintendent of schools reasoned with her and regular prayer meetings were held over her after school.

In the later meetings the revivalist made it clear that he expected a donation at the close of the appointed two weeks. While he toiled earnestly in the Lord's vineyard, he evidently had little faith in his employer as paymaster. He said he wanted to carry away with him some tangible remembrance of the "season of refreshment." He announced that on the last night he would stand at the door to shake hands with his beloved flock and would like to have each one write on a slip of paper a favorite quotation from the Bible and slip it into an envelope with whatever contribution the spirit moved him to make. He assured them that the spiritual value of the scriptural quotations would be far above the price of rubies, but he did not allow his audience to forget that while man did not live by bread alone he *did* have to have more than the crumbs from a rich man's table.

One of the committee members in charge of the meetings was with the revivalist when he opened the envelopes. The man tore them open eagerly, took out the money, and threw the rest away without a glance at the precious bits of scripture.

It was a harsh experience for the little community.

The "Big Four" and Accreditation

Mr. Brown, the new principal, was a very young man, fresh from the university. He was of slender build, with a small head which he was inclined to thrust forward as he talked. He had a smooth face and small black eyes that moved restlessly from object to object. He was quick in motion and too quick in making decisions. He was alert in manner and cordial in greeting. He was intensely earnest and took life very seriously indeed.

Young people accept any change naturally. They regretted the loss of Miss McClellan but they turned submissively to her successor and everything started off well.

In addition to my other classes I was assigned astronomy, since my store of knowledge consisted of the names and locations of four or five constellations, one more than the other teachers knew. That term I became a second Diogenes in the diligence of my search, for with lantern and a chart I explored the heavens for constellations and planets.

In this class I encountered a new set of pupils. They were juniors and among them was a group of boys different from the ruling element in the senior class. They were not remarkable as students and were always ready for a frolic. If fun didn't come their way naturally, they invented some. As they were restless, full of energy, and ready to take a joke and to give one, I found new trials. I learned a great deal from my experience with this class.

The Niles High School was a strong one and the pupils drove

me hard, but it had never been on the University of Michigan's accredited list. Very few of its graduates had gone to college but this year the "big four," consisting of George Cooper, Frank Russel, Dan Alton, and Edward Hosmer, were all planning to go. To make it possible for them to enter without an examination, Mr. Thomas had made application for a committee to be sent from the university to examine the school.

Until the last moment, it is never known who is to come but I knew that mathematics was one of the important subjects and no matter who the examiners were, my algebra classes were bound to be inspected carefully. I dreaded the ordeal, and when I learned that Professor Olney, head of the mathematics department, and Professor D'Ooge of the Latin department would visit my classes the next day, I was panic stricken.

Courtesy: Michigan Historical Collection, Bentley Historical Library, The University of Michigan

Benjamin Leonard D'Ooge   **Edward Olney**

The next morning there was a great algebraic commotion in my room before school. Everyone was eager to put props under all his weak points. We moved over to the assembly room. The two professors were ushered in and took their seats on the platform. All eyes were upon them. Men having such power as to hold the reputation of the whole school in their hands must be mighty indeed. Each spoke but I heard not a word.

Mr. Brown brought Professor Olney to my second hour algebra class and seated him on the platform. He was a gentle mannered, low voiced, kindly old gentleman and immediately I felt perfectly at ease with him. I even found him so pleasant that I forgot what he was there for, until suddenly I remembered that it was he who had concocted all those hard examples in geometrical progression that had kept me on the rack for weeks. At this realization I experienced a severe attack of stagefright.

I sent the class to the board, but my voice failed and although I walked up and down the room to cover my embarrassment and to gain possession of my faculties, it was several minutes before I could gain strength enough to assign the problems. I then returned to the platform. Blessed be the memory of Professor Olney, for he turned to me and said, "How long have you been teaching?"

"Only a few months," I answered.

"That's why you are so frightened then. But never mind. I didn't know much about math at your age and probably didn't know as much about teaching as you do. Now just let me teach this class and you watch. Perhaps you can learn something from an old man who has taught math for forty years."

What an experience it was to watch him handle that class. The boys and girls were not at all disturbed when he took charge. They were on their mettle to do their best and I was surprised to see them recite better than they did for me. I had thought a question should be made difficult, but this man had an entirely different way. First he put them completely at ease. Instead of trying to confuse them he put his questions clearly and logically so that often a pupil who knew very little about a particular problem at the beginning would gradually work his way into a clear understanding. He told them nothing but by skillful questioning he made each one use his mind until he mastered the situation. Every one of us was surprised when the bell struck, ending the hour.

Professor D'Ooge came after Professor Olney to go with him to hear a Latin class:

"I'm having a good time here. Isn't your next class algebra, too, Miss Cushman?" I replied that it was.

"Then I think I'll stay right here. I've forgotten most of my Latin anyway and wouldn't be of much help to you."

When Professor Olney realized that my senior class included the four boys for whose sake the school was being examined, he went after them in a manner very different from that of the previous class. He hammered them with questions, and he insisted upon rapid work and did not try to make things easy.

I felt more at ease with this class, and I was proud as Frank

Russel stood up against the hard quizzing without the slightest discomfort. George and Edward and Dan were not far behind. Anna and Jennie were both shining lights. In fact, I was very proud of each one.

During my one free period, Professor Olney spent most of that hour discussing my work. He encouraged me, said pleasant things about what I had already done, criticized some methods and gave me much food for thought. It was an eventful day in my life and exerted a great influence on my future teaching.

Both the Latin and Greek classes had distinguished themselves, for the "big four" constituted the entire Anabasis class and a large part of the Virgil class. Other reports were not as encouraging and everybody waited in great anxiety for the official communication from the university. In a small town the high school is an important center of interest and its affairs common talk, so for two weeks the visitation and the possible failure of the school to be put upon the diploma list were discussed at the post office, on street corners, and in every parlor.

When the letter came from the university, it was read to the teachers at a meeting held for that purpose. It began by making severe criticism of certain faults, commended other things and ended by saying that, after much discussion, they had decided to accept without examination the four boys who were planning to attend the university in the fall because the committee felt that these individuals were prepared for college work. By this action the school would be placed on the diploma list for one year; if it desired permanent relations another committee would visit again the next spring.

Every teacher breathed a deep sigh of relief and secretly set standards for better work the coming term.

I went into my room, threw open the windows wide to the mildness of the spring and sat in semidarkness, languidly enjoying the breath and promise of the season. There was a whir in my ear, a waft of air on my cheeks, and a gentle thud on the floor. "Could it be a bat this early?" I wondered as stepped over to turn up the light.

In the middle of the floor lay a daintly bunch of hepaticas and spring beauties. I pressed them to my face and drank deep of their woodsy fragrance. I was shocked by the realization that flowers were growing in the woods all around me and I had been totally unaware.

I went to the window to catch a glimpse of the messenger but of course he had gone but there was no doubt in my mind as to who he was. No one but Frank Russel cared as I did for the woods and the flowers and our talks about them had been frequent.

June days brought sunshine, and roses and commencement. This occasion in Niles was an important event. The exercises were held in the evening in the half opera house which saw all public gatherings of moment. This year each one of the eighteen graduates was to have a place on the program, and a large crowd was expected.

Miss McClellan had always had charge of the stage arrangements but this year they were turned over to me. It was the duty of the juniors to decorate the hall and the stage. Garlands of green, mingled with the red and white class colors, festooned the railings of the balcony and framed the stage, the front of which was banked with ferns and palms. The stiff rows of chairs for teachers and students on the platform were abolished. Instead, sofas, chairs, and tables were arranged there as for a drawing room. Cut flowers and plants were on table and piano, and when the teachers and pupils took their places it seemed more like a dignified social function in a private home rather than a school exercise.

The girls were all dressed in white and each carried a sheaf of pink roses. How proud I felt of each one, as I sat there with diplomas tied with ribbon on the table beside me. The boys, with their serious and almost grownup expressions, sat almost rigidly in their seats. I felt as though I knew personally the struggles, the disappointments, and the successes of each young graduate.

In the general and informal socializing that followed the secretary of the board came to me and said, "Miss Cushman, I am directed by the Board to say that you have *again* been elected principal of the Niles High School." I had been offered the position when Mr. Brown was in serious difficulties previously, but had refused because I was certain that matters could be remedied and they were. Mr. Brown, who was standing nearby, hastened to add, "It's really alright this time. I've resigned in earnest and start my job in the business world tomorrow. I've discovered that teaching is not my field, and I know the school will be in good hands."

I was pleased and grateful that now the position was mine honorably and I knew that I was much better prepared for the responsibility than I could have been in the spring.

The year I became principal, my father, who was ill and unable to work, and my mother and twin sisters moved to Niles from Dowagiac, thus making our combined expenses much less. The twins entered high school that year and were in some of my classes.

During the preceding two years the charge of the assembly room had fallen to me for a few hours or a few days at a time, so the responsibility was not entirely new. But to follow the policy of another and to keep things going in a way already defined is one thing; to shape the policy according to new needs and in harmony with my own personality was another.

Again, the courage of youth took me into this new work with confidence. In the following two years I learned many lessons, some of them through dealing wisely with a given situation, some of them through failure.

Perhaps my most serious mistake was in depending too much on personal influence. The boys and girls liked me and usually could be brought to any desired course of action when they knew my wishes, but that method of discipline is not of the highest order. School in those days was 150 students in the assembly room, all under my responsibility. My classes met in recitation in front of a platform in front of the large room, while the back rows were filled with students who were supposed to be studying. I was an enthusiastic teacher and too often became so absorbed in my teaching that I utterly forgot the pupils in the back of the room.

One day the superintendent came in and, feeling the responsibility of having placed me in this new position, he remarked on the noisiness of the room. I truthfully had not been aware of the confusion but I turned to the students and reminded them that they were not taking very good care of themselves. Their response was immediate. The superintendent smiled and said, "Well, I guess the school belongs to you yet."

These years in Niles laid the foundation in habits of study upon which the superstructure of all later achievement was built. The second year did not make such demands upon my time in simply keeping up with the class so there was leisure for other studies. Although I had read Horace and Tacitus during the five months of college, there had been no opportunity for Virgil. Beginning at first alone, but finding it somewhat uncertain work, I finally asked the help of the superintendent. With occasional recitations progress was more rapid so I read that winter the twelve books of Virgil.

The habits formed during those days have held, and through all the years of teaching, and even to the present moment, I have never been without some line of systematic study or literary work. Often the time is limited to a few minutes a day, but I have never let it go entirely. The very fact of holding to the idea that one is going to study counts for much, for when the opportunity offers the intellectual muscles are ready. Latin, Greek, German, French, mathematics, history and general literature — whatever I know of them has all been gained by patient, persistent study with little outside help. The progress is slow, uncomfortable, and discouraging, but it will produce results, and to the hungry, "part of a loaf is better than no loaf at all."

I spent five years in that school, teaching almost every subject in the curriculum and working hard to keep up with my classes. During those five years I served my apprenticeship. The young teacher of today gets her training more easily although she is bound to miss many things traveling the royal road.

Those days of desperate struggle for the mastery of what I must teach others brought a nearness to the needs of a student that can not come in any other way. Through long years of teaching subjects grown almost mechanically familiar, the memory has always held of those long night vigils and the struggle to make the page yield its truth to me. When a boy or girl has failed to see what is almost axiomatic, my mind goes back to my own difficulties over perhaps the very same thing. My study table with its books, the furniture, the pictures on the wall, the glow of the lamp appear with photographic distinctness. The noise of the street, the voices of children in the yard, even the perfume of the blossoming vines about the window are a part of the memory. As it all comes before me, sympathy for the young girl, who no longer seems myself, makes for patience with the youth now struggling with the same vexations.

At the beginning of my fifth year, the superintendent, who had been so long in charge of the Niles schools, was called to a better position. His successor was not equal to the duties and that year was a difficult one. He was a well-meaning man which is damning him with faint praise. One incident will do to reveal the type of man. In a small town the playing of practical jokes is a rominent source of amusement. Among other tricks, a group of high school boys one night changed the wheel of the superintendent's high buggy. One big wheel and one small one on each side, alternating its position, gave a peculiar rocking motion to the buggy. He drove that buggy in that condition for several days oblivious of the change.

Within my own province, as with many other teachers, the change of superintendents was not seriously felt for some time, but the general discipline of the building weakened and it was with increasing difficulty that any of us maintained the old standards. There was disorder in the halls, the waves of which broke often at my threshold, and it took more energy each day to still the troubled waters. All this combined to make me willing to think of a change. It finally resulted in my accepting the position as preceptress of the high school in Marshall, Michigan.

For eleven years the school in Marshall had been under the administration of Henry French as superintendent. He had put the stamp of his strong personality upon the entire organization and had gathered around him an unusually competent corps of teachers. The preceptress whom I followed had been there for nine years, was adored by the pupils, and held almost in reverence by the people of the city. She was not an easy person to follow. The school, however, realized that she was compelled to leave because of her health and accepted me, probably with critical comparisons, but nevertheless wholeheartedly.

Everything went splendidly until spring, when Mr. French was called to a larger city. It soon became evident that I had jumped from the frying pan into the fire. Henry French's successor brought troubles and vexations far greater than those from which I had fled. Mr. French was broadminded and possessed some confidence in human nature, and best of all had a sense of humor. He even saw the amusing side of education and could point his finger pointedly upon the foibles of faddism and too much coddling.

Mr. French believed in his teachers, and the corps when I joined it certainly was worthy of every confidence. The new man believed in no one, either teachers or pupils. He was sure that girls and boys were always on mischief bent, and when he saw two or three teachers together, he knew they were deeply plotting his overthrow, when probably they were not concerned with him at all.

His whole policy was revealed to us in a teachers' meeting which he called soon after his arrival. Certain things that he said made such an impression upon me that I shall not go far astray by enclosing in quotation marks his words as I remember them. The spirit of them is certainly retained. "I wish you all to understand that I have come here to be superintendent, and that I shall *be* superintendent. It is your duty as subordinates to obey me absolutely and to carry out my wishes in every particular."

One final memory of these years deserves mention. A very good friend in Niles and a man later known quite well throughout the state was E.C. Dana. He had been one of the early newspaper editors in Niles and always active in town affairs. He was a man, small of stature, sunny by nature, thoughtful of everybody, helpful to any who needed help, friend of all who would accept the free gift of his friendship and the loving service that went with it. He had an eager, active mind — a heart big enough to encompass first a great suffering humanity and then have room for all the jokes and joys that spring up in the pathway of such a soul. Many are the remembrances of his kindness.

Some years after I left Niles the papers were full of some of the odd titles used to address this man and the Post Offices were ingenious in identifying him. Some of the addresses on letters were: "To the Smallest Man, but the Largest Hearted in Niles," "To the Charming Little Man with the Great Big Soul," or even "Keyboard Bellows Dana," evidently bearing a joke understood by the sender only, or "Literary Dana." The town was often omitted. Letters reached him with the simple address, "The Prince of Entertainers," and that he was.

On to Grand Rapids
and Marriage

A new opportunity was offered to me as assistant to the principal, Samuel G. Milner, of the Union School in Grand Rapids, Michigan. The school was on the west side of the Grand River and at that time was, in the estimation of the eastsiders, the usual "across the river" or "across the railroad tracks" neighborhood. The Union was one of the two high schools but it offered only two years of high school work, the pupils after that going to the Central. Mr. Milner had been principal for eight years. Besides the responsibility for the entire building, he had charge of the upper study room in which the eighth grade, added to the two years of high school, brought the number of pupils to about 125. He also did some teaching. He had never had adequate assistance and there had been no one to whom he could confidently leave the room when his duties as principal took him elsewhere. He had been in the habit of calling in a recitation teacher for any few minutes of necessary supervision, returning to the room as soon as possible.

In my classroom I found new problems but they were nothing compared with those of the study room. When Mr. Milner threw open my door it was the signal for me to take charge or pretend to, for really I was of no more account than a fly buzzing upon the ceiling. The lift of the principal's finger, a glance from his kindly eye was sufficient to keep the school in order, but no assistant had had that power. The room had long indulged in mad frolics whenever he left it, but he had no realization of the extent of the disorder.

As soon as the door closed behind him the uproar began. Words were of no avail for they could not be heard; reproving looks never found a mark. At first I took it as a personal affront but soon realized that they were not giving me a single thought. I began to study the situation and to seek a remedy, for it never occurred to me that I should not eventually conquer. At last I evolved a plan. The next day I hovered near the door and when I heard Mr. Milner's steps approaching, I met him in the study room and made for the boys' side of the room. Right before the door closed, I shouted "Boys you haven't played fair with me."

Most boys will pause at such an accusation. Taking advantage of an instant's quiet I expressed my opinion of their actions, and the language was plain enough to reach the dullest boy. It did make some slight impression. Since I had been hired on my reputation as a disciplinarian, it was time that I make some progress. At my urgent request, Mr. Milner agreed to stay out of the room a little longer each day and give me a chance to make my authority felt. It was a long and hard battle, but as I became acquainted with individual pupils there was a steady gain until eventually the school recognized my authority, but that badge of power never could be laid aside.

Courtesy: Grand Rapids Public Library Michigan Room

Grand Rapids Union School (c. 1890)

Grand Rapids then and for many years after dominated the furniture business of the United States. Most of the plants were on the west side. Here, as I remember, were located the Phoenix Furniture Co., Whiddicomb Furniture Co., Grand Rapids Schoolseat Co., now American Seating Co., Grand Rapids Chair Co., (one of the Foote boys was in the Union School), and the Grand Rapids Veneer Works. Several of the executives of these famous factories had their homes on the west side and the children were in our school. Other boys and girls were from homes of especially skilled workmen, others from those of day laborers, sweepers, and others. In fact we must have had a cross- section of midwestern life in the early 1880s.

Had I been more mature, more sensitive to the challenge of the subject, here was a chance to learn, first hand, much of the beginnings of the labor movement in this country. Here I had my first glimpse of the attitude of mind that controls labor unions, strikes, and the fierce antagonism to so-called capital. Through individual boys and the general attitude of their class was revealed their belief or perhaps their instinct that the world and everything in it was against them; that they must fight each step of the way, and that any attempt at friendliness must be treated with suspicion and looked at with caution less there be an attempt to take unfair advantage in some way.

In spite of the fact that my father had been a mechanic earning much less in proportion than most of these fathers were earning, I was unable to understand their attitude. Now-a-days, the power seems to lie in the other direction and Labor is as unyielding and blind to the welfare of the entire country as management used to be. At this later date, at which time I am now writing, I often wonder if the same spirit that in these years has produced so much labor trouble was not the unconscious power that gave me so much trouble in this school at first.

Echoes of ideas from home were evident and it was easy to see the eager pushing forward toward a betterment of conditions and the attendant jealousy of those ahead of them.

Every new "ism" that seemed to promise the overthrow of "capital" and the arbitrary distribution of this world's goods upon a purely numerical basis found ready lodgment. The whole attitude was most puzzling to me.

As I came to know the young people better and developed a real affection for them (some of my lifelong friends date from these years), their position became clearer, and while I never came to agree entirely with their point of view, I did gain some slight understanding for their bitterness and suspicion. These glimpses left me with a wider charity for all whose opinions might differ from mine and a keener appreciation of some things that made life hard for those who have nothing to depend upon but their daily toil and nothing to inspire them but the hourly wage.

These young people were quick to learn, but only a few of them had ambitions beyond completing the course at the Union School, and many fell short of that. A few went across the river to Central High and were graduated, while an occasional one went on to college. When later the eleventh grade was added at Union, many continued who would have stopped at the necessary change of school.

This school was always a difficult one and gave me my hardest years of teaching. I was often discouraged. At the time I was not conscious of unusual strain, but evidence of it shows to this day. A good sleeper, I rarely am conscious of a dream, but one nightmare occasionally haunts me. I am back in that assembly room trying to bring order out of chaos.

The personal life cannot be entirely separated from the professional. Let this be the apology for the following paragraphs.

When I went to Grand Rapids, I made arrangements to room with Mary Haskell, who had already taught a year at Union. We took a small sitting room with larger adjoining bedroom, with board at the Brinsmaids', well known as the best boarding place on the west side, and it deserved all the praise bestowed on it. We paid the fabulous sum of $2.50 each week. It really was a home, with Mr. and Mrs. Brinsmaid the heads of the family. If they have not found a high place in heaven, then justice has not been served. They had about eight boarders, half of whom came from the outside for their meals. Among the latter were Mr. Milner and Edwin Barry, who roomed together.

On the evening of our arrival, the two men came to supper a little late and took seats at the opposite end of the table. They left immediately afterward so our only contact was in the general conversation. It was revealed later that as they went down the steps, Ed remarked, "Sam, that's the woman you are going to marry."

"Possibly" was the answer.

My diary for that evening registered my own "love at first sight." There is the record for all that it is worth.

Samuel G. Milner (c. 1890)

Although the young people at school did not pay much attention to my efforts at discipline, in other ways they were more attentive. They early observed what they considered marked attention on the part of their principal to the new teacher. They knew that for years he had gone back and forth alone. Now they discovered that he frequently accompanied the new assistant and, as we learned later, used to congregate to watch us go away together. They approved from the first and gave us their "God bless you" before we realized that we wanted it. But they were wiser than we in seeing the end from the beginning and were impatient at our slowness in arriving at a conclusion which they reached at a bound. At last, not entirely for the sake of carrying out their wishes, Mr. Milner and I agreed with their judgment.

We reached our decision early in the fall of my second year in Grand Rapids, and planned to be married the following summer. As the days wore on, however, we saw no reason why we should wait. No matter when we might marry, my determination was fixed to continue teaching for a time. Both of us carried heavy family obligations, which made it necessary for us to earn as much as possible. Besides, it had been no part of Mr. Milner's early intention to make teaching his life work. He was headed for medicine, but up to that time conditions had made it impossible for him to renounce a sure salary for a new venture.

In those days, the early 1880's, few women continued teaching after marriage and it was bound to create some comment, which Mr. Milner naturally dreaded, but I insisted upon continuing my work. Our friends understood and the others were unimportant.

We were married January 3, 1883, in my mother's home in Niles. To please her, we had a large but simple wedding. We would have preferred just a family ceremony, but after the evening wedding, we had our way.

Ed Barry had given up his part of the apartment in Grand Rapids and the three rooms were adjusted to light housekeeping. We went immediately there from the late train. We did not look much like a bridal pair. Mr. Milner carried a well-packed basket for our breakfast. Our apartment was but a few blocks from the station so we walked. This was before the days of taxis, and hacks were always an abomination to me. Nearly a week of the holiday vacation remained; our friends considerately left us alone, and that was our honeymoon.

Our return to school was a festive one. The pupils had decorated the room, adorned our respective chairs, and piled many loving gifts on the desk. It was a reception from the hearts of these children who two years ago had seemed to me to be such barbarians. From that time things went on as usual even to the children continuing to call me Miss Cushman.

Ann Arbor:
An Education Continues

For two and a half years after our marriage, our lives were busy in school affairs. We had saved a little money, and decided that the time had come for my husband to start his medical work. We resigned from the school and with the faith of the "fowls of the air" departed for Ann Arbor.

I had no intention of living in idleness. Through the endorsement of Professor Olney, who had been so good to me in Niles, and Professor Isaac Demmon, a college friend of my husband's, a position to teach algebra and review arithmetic in the Ann Arbor High School was given to me (September 1885).

The high school was practically a preparatory school for the university, and there was a dominating number of students from towns whose schools did not prepare for college. Consequently the organization stressed classroom work and little time was given to activities familiar to most schools. There was a general assembly once a week for simple chapel services and for such announcements as concerned the whole student body. We were really a recitation mill grinding out thoroughly good college material. Our recitations began at eight and ran until one, and as far as I can remember there was no place for studying at the school. The standard of scholarship was high, but classes were too large and the teaching force and salaries were kept to the minimum. Salaries could be kept low because of the desirability of teaching in a college town where the teachers could also attend classes for credit.

When I entered the Ann Arbor High School, it was the custom to address the pupils as "Mister" or "Miss." I had not been used to that and did not like it. It seemed to me absurd to address a youth not yet arrived at long trousers as "Mr. Brown" or a girl of the same age as "Miss Jones," so I did the natural thing and said "John" or "Mary" or "Jane," as the case might be. Some of those boys and girls have since become teachers and have told me that nothing I did at first won them so completely as that one thing. One of them said, "When you called us Genevieve and Mary, my sister and I felt at home in your room and glad when algebra recitation time came. We have followed the same custom in our own teaching even though, as in your case, we were the only teachers in the school who did it."

It often happened that a mature young man, markedly older than the majority of the class came to the Ann Arbor High School for belated preparation for college. He, of course, was always addressed as "Mister" because he would have been so addressed anywhere. Simply, I did the thing in school that would have been natural to do elsewhere.

The class in arithmetic fell to my lot and numbered fifty four, so there was little opportunity to judge individual results or to do good teaching. At the end of the term I told the superintendent my plan was to pass all who were five feet tall. When he later said that he had never seen the subject taught better, it did not seem to me a compliment, only evidence of the poor work of all of us. Later experience added to the conviction that no subject was so poorly taught as arithmetic.

Since my classes were over at 1:00 the first year, it was a great temptation to matriculate and pursue more knowledge, officially, but this did not seem wise, since I was doing a great deal of tutoring and needed to be free when necessary. But even if one were not a regular student, opportunities were abundant. Classes were open to visitors, and each year I selected one or two in English or history. Regular attendance upon lectures, systematic study, and the run of the library made for me an intellectual paradise.

To climb the narrow stairways leading from story to story, to wander unmolested in and out among the shelves even with hand never lifted to a book, but searching the titles hungrily, was a joy in itself. To go with Professor Demmon to the Shakespeare section, which he had gathered book by book, to sweep the range from facsimile of first folio (there was no original there then) to a miniature modern edition, to read inscriptions in association copies, gave me my first knowledge of rare books. But best of all was to ask this Shakespeare lover some question on the Bacon-Shakespeare controversy raging at the time, and see the scorn gather in his scholarly face, followed by a rapid-fire tirade against the absurdity.

Usually the time in the library was spent in study. An historical note, a reference to novel, poem, or essay, started a search that ran in many directions until the library seemed honeycombed with the one idea. The huntsman with his gun, the animal lover with camera, the bird lover with field glass, steal through the woods with bated breath. There is something of the same excitement in pursuing a single idea through the labyrinth of a great library. One follows up a reference confident of soon running the idea to earth, only to find the trail empty of all he sought. Nothing daunted, he starts upon another scent, follows it from stack to stack, from book to book, through index after index until at last the game is in the bag, and he is off on another trail.

There were larger libraries than this and in later years I came to know the greatest university library in the same intimate way, but this one at Ann Arbor first "opened its heart to me, therefore, I love it."

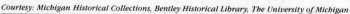

Courtesy: Michigan Historical Collections, Bentley Historical Library, The University of Michigan

Ann Arbor High School (c. 1880)

Ann Arbor was a beautiful town in the years of 1885-88. It still is, but then the woods and rolling countryside were almost a part of the campus. Many were the hours we spent outdoors as we followed miles and miles of beautiful roads that tempted us in every direction. They led over gentle hills, through cool valleys, along the winding river and across wide level bottom lands. The roadsides were an ever- shifting scene of beauty. In the spring the crisp green was sprinkled with pink and white blossoms — all roads were bordered by quantities of wild roses that draped themselves over every fence and stump. Fields and roadsides yellowed in the summer sunshine, deepening through August red of sumac to the blaze of autumn splendor, and then fading to the white and black and gray of the winter landscape. Each change was beautiful, each shifting scene a picture to remember.

My husband and I wandered close to the river's brim, or climbed the hills or went for a brisk constitutional over level road, or on a picnic with the Demmons. The evenings spent in study often found us at midnight, weary of books, oppressed by four walls, and cramped. A plunge into the night air was like one's morning bath for refreshment. The country was so near, and when on our favorite walk out Washtenaw Avenue we reached Tuomy's Hill, we were far beyond the edge of town, in the silence of moonlight or starlight. *(On Tuomy's Hill was Tuomy's House, now the headquarters of the Historical Society of Michigan.)*

My husband found many of his former professors still occupying the same chairs and several of his classmates and fraternity brothers (Alpha Delta Phi) added to the faculty. These and all their families greeted him cordially, accepted his wife, and opened doors wide to us. Society in Ann Arbor in those days was like one great family, and like all interesting families its members were possessed of marked individuality. Conversation was definitely not a lost art, and whether few or many were gathered together there was always good talk, making "a world where ideas were current and speech was wine." Each man had his special line of work but not so highly specialized that he could not find interest in what others were doing.

The women were equally interesting. Most of them had traveled and in those travels had devoted themselves to art, music, and shopping for characteristic curios of the places visited. They were alert conversationalists and good homemakers. Only a few possess much if anything beyond the moderate salary of a professor. One wife summed up their contentment in a few words: "We don't even know we're poor unless someone from outside comes and tells us." Taste, order, and thoughtful care was everywhere manifest. There was no mistaking one home for another or confusing the dominant interests. In one would be treasures that would be the envy of the antiquarian — quaint pieces of silver, rare old English prints in period frames, china, old mahogany rich with the deepening dye of time and even richer in association, such as Professor Demmon's old desk with its memories of Blennerhassett where it once did service, or the beautiful bookcase from the home of the university's first president. Another home told of long residence in Athens, while another was equally eloquent of Rome. When upon the library shelves one might discover rare editions and from his hiding place behind a row of books the owner, half ashamed of his extravagance, would shyly draw out a volume long since out of print and very scarce, there could be no doubt about his hobby. Such homes cannot be made to order; they must be as these were, the natural manifestation of the taste and culture of the people themselves. Money cannot buy it and there is no substitute for refinement.

Mrs. Demmon kept open house on Sunday afternoon and evening. No invitations were issued and friends were welcome whenever the spirit moved them to come. Supper was served at a regular hour and the hostess never knew whether to expect ten or twenty. It became a regular thing for us to go there Sunday nights, Mrs. Demmon insisting that she needed us to help when numbers became unexpectantly large. I suspected the soundness of her excuse but the temptation was too great to resist.

These Sunday evenings were among the pleasantest remembrances of Ann Arbor. In summer dinner was often served on the porch or under the great oaks, wonderful trees, each an imposing individual. In winter we gathered around small tables in the living room where flowers, an open fire, rare books, and interesting people combined to make a distinctive atmosphere. Sometimes the men wandered by twos or threes across the hall to the book-lined study whence tantalizing snatches of talk floated back to make one long to hear the rest. The company was never twice the same; literature, history, classics, romance languages, law, medicine, art, philosophy, and science, represented by such men as Elisha Jones, Dr. W.J. Herdman, Dr.

Victor C. Vaughan, Albert Pattengill, brother of our "High School Pat," Judson Pattengill, Professor Walter who was lost on "La Bourgone," Richard Hudson, Dr Warthen, and Charles Gayley. The latter was one of the younger men who was already making a name for himself locally as a poet. He will be remembered as the author of the two popular Michigan songs "The Yellow and the Blue" and "Goddess of the Inland Seas." Professor Pattengill and he, in spite of the difference in age, were good friends and the older man was greatly interested in Gayley's poetry. He had a friend associated with *Harper's* and thought he could bring the attention of the editors of the magazine to his protege. He sent a bundle of Gayley's poems to this friend and waited anxiously for results. They came back in a letter saying "Our pigeon holes are full of things as good." Mr. Pattengill flashed back: "Why, in thunder, then, don't you publish some of it?" He is not the only one who has felt the same about rejected manuscripts.

All this was like heady wine to me, for it was my first intimate association with people whose pursuits were purely intellectual.

Perhaps I never worked harder then the three years in Ann Arbor. The second year the enrollment increased and extra classes had to be provided and I taught until three o'clock. I also continued my tutoring, until during the last months of our time there I was teaching twelve hours a day. I had perfect health and unlimited energy and was not conscious of any great strain. My whole ambition was to finish without a debt, and that we did. I suppose the fact that we were having interesting contacts with fine people, a social life that I had never known existed, and entrance into homes where standards were high and of a scholarly nature gave the strength and resiliency to carry me through.

When my husband was given his medical degree, President Angell did a very gracious thing. He remembered that Mr. Milner had been in the first class to be graduated under his presidency many years before. The diplomas for the larger classes were usually given in bundles to the deans of the different schools. When it came to my husband's class, President Angell took out one diploma and at the appropriate time rose and presented it, personally, with a pleasant official remark.

After his internship my husband returned to Grand Rapids to open his office. I awaited the end of the term before joining him.

In many ways these years at Ann Arbor had a lasting influence on me, both personally and as a teacher. It set standards for a home and showed me the possibility of gathering about oneself things of real value even with limited means. It gave me a clearer view of what the really best things are and seeing matters in the right proportions. Up to the time of going to Ann Arbor, my social contacts had been very limited. There I learned much of the true value of living surroundings and much of the amenities of social intercourse, a valuable education in itself for any teacher.

Back to Grand Rapids
and Central High School

U on my arrival in Grand Rapids we went to the Livingston Hotel to stay until we could find a suitable house, for my teaching days were over. From now on I was to revel in the position of wife and housekeeper. But the Saturday before the opening of school my dream of domesticity was shattered.

The head of the English department in the Central High School had been ill since early spring. At the last moment she had asked for an extension of her leave for another two months. Would I substitute for that period? The teacher in me sprang eagerly to the opportunity. The only obstacle was my husband's pride—and this was most important in 1888 and to be expected. This was overcome because the arrangement was only temporary and the emergency in the school crucial. On Monday morning I went into that school for a prospective two months and remained twelve years.

These years in this high school with its varying experiences and the association with its fine corps of teachers molded me into the kind of teacher I finally found myself to be. The principal, William Albert Greeson, was one of the exceptionally strong principals under whom I have been privileged to work. We had known him before going to Ann Arbor, but living on opposite sides of the river we had little association outside of school affairs. Now the acquaintance ripened into a personal friendship which only death severed.

It is not easy to describe the qualities that made for Mr.

Greeson's success, but the outstanding one was that he was always himself, never a pedagogue. He went about the building in his usual manner, took no pains to walk silently, and wore no carpet slippers. He never was in a hurry, never flustered, and teacher and pupil found each case that was brought to his attention treated as it were the only one for the day. Pupils never changed attitude at his approach, although they were sure of their just desserts if found in the wrong.

Two instances illustrate the naturalness of his manner. One day just before noon he came into my session room, hat in hand. With a twinkle in his eye and in a voice audible to all said, "Schuyler Graves has an appointment over in the alley to fight a boy and I'm going along to referee. I'll be back before luncheon." Schuyler followed him out and the school took it all as a matter of course.

Another day he appeared at my recitation room door asking in a pefectly natural manner, "Have you any money?" The *Britannica* man is here with the new volume and I haven't enough to pay him." I handed him my pocketbook. Had I, too, been penniless, no doubt he would have appealed to the class and they, doubtless, would have taken up a collection, had it been necessary.

It was during these years that I first realized with some clearness the place that training of the imagination should have in all good teaching. To little children the world of the imagination is vivid and real. They need no explanation of *Alice in Wonderland*, *Peter Pan*, or *Wind in the Willows*. One can make a remark as fanciful as one wishes and the child will enter into the spirit of it. They are at home in the make-believe world. Later, in the upper grades, self-consciousness steps in and drives the imagination into the background and eventually silences it. There comes a time, it seems to me, when it has to be aroused and perhaps its existence justified.

In the English history class one day, we were discussing the Arthurian legends. Enthusiasm led me to speak as though the events in the stories of *The Coming of Arthur* and of the good sword Excalibur were as real as those of the Revolutionary War. One of the boys interrupted, a bit scornfully:

"Mrs. Milner, do you really believe those stories?"

"Of course I believe them. I wouldn't fail to believe them for anything. But understand me, I believe them with my imagination, not entirely with my reason."

The boy understood.

In this school I learned that whoever teaches history and misses its poetry and romance has failed even though he trains classes thoroughly in constitutional history. He who teaches English and fails to make some heart beat faster at the reading of a great piece of literature or thrill to the perfectly turned sentence offers but the husks. Many mature people insist that they have no love of poetry and cannot read it. This may be because at the right time there was no one to open the enchanted realm. To be sure, there may be exceptions but they must be like the woman who "saw no Mt. Blanc because there was no Mt. Blanc within her." But usually there is a time when the whole nature is attuned to this form of expression. Then the great poets, if given the opportunity, may speak with lasting results.

One day I was reading a selection of which I was particularly fond. When I had finished a boy asked, "Mrs. Milner, how does one get to care for such things as you do?"

I was standing at the time and made three emphatic steps toward him speaking a word at each step, "Read, Read, Read."

This boy was so interested in science that he thought nothing else worth much consideration. The boy was Burton E. Livingston, long on the faculty of the Johns Hopkins University, an authority in his branch of botany, and a man who has held important positions in scientific organizations. He told me later that my words had sent him to reading and that this love of books had rounded out his equipment so that he became a much better scientist than he could have been without the knowledge of general literature, and a much better writer than he could have in his own field without this wider reading. Too many scientists remain merely scientists and lose the broadening influence that literary culture gives. This he had attained without lessening in the least his scientific achievements.

There remains little of continuity in my remembrance of various experiences in this school. Many were the lessons learned and the problems with students faced. Many of my lifelong friends grew out of the troubles that brought us into contact in this school, and a few might be worth mentioning.

There is a saying that "a good teacher always should have one blind eye." The teacher who is always on the watch for disorder and infraction of rules will not often be disappointed. This I found out in my contact with Gilbert White, a younger brother of Stewart Edward White, who had also been my student. Gilbert was one of the boys I liked especially. Nevertheless he was troublesome and I had to call him to order time and time again. One day he said to me, "Mrs. Milner, you find fault with me all the time. You see everything that I do but other boys do the same thing and you never see them." His remark gave me pause. After a few moments thinking I answered, "Gilbert, I believe you are right. You have disturbed me so often that I suppose you got on my nerves. I don't intentionally watch you, but I can't help seeing everything you do. I am wrong in nagging you and I will try to stop it. For one week, I will not speak to you once in reproof. Perhaps in that way I can do away with my supersensitiveness, but I'll expect you to keep yourself pretty well in order, too, for that time."

By the time the week was up Gilbert had settled into his normal place in my consciousness and no longer disturbed me. We became real friends, which friendship continued over these many years and gave me many interesting hours with him at different times in Paris, where he had gained for himself a reputation as an artist. He had shown much talent along this line in Grand Rapids, where he had made some of the illustrations for the *Olympian*, the student annual, and gave a very fine chalk talk at the Delta Gamma Psi banquet in 1898. Some of his pictures made in Paris have found their way to America, among them a memorial to the fallen soldiers of Oklahoma — a large mural for the Capitol Building. I saw this when I visited him at his Paris studio one year before it was completed. I also attended his wedding and reception, both in his studio.

Another "problem" that turned out successfully was a boy named Cornelius Hoffius, who one day openly defied me. Nothing could be more of a challenge to me—and here was my opportunity to make a great mistake, but some angel must have stood over me and guided my thoughts and actions. Anger flamed inside but I only looked at the boy for an instant, turned to the school, made my closing announcements and dismissed the room.

Later I called him in to discuss the matter—and in this and further talks I learned much about the boy. He had fought every inch of his way in life against heavy odds. He had worked to clothe himself ever since he was a little fellow, and since he had been in high school had paid board at home. He sold papers on the street at noon and after school and carried an early morning route as well. His haste on this particular day was due to the necessity for getting to a certain street corner with his paper in time to catch the noon rush and to hold his stand against ambitious competitors. He even had worked up a good business at the Soldiers Home. I found that he not only sold papers but he read them. He knew what was going on in the world and had his opinions about political affairs. On inquiry I found he was doing good work in all his subjects but no teacher could get near him. He wrote exceedingly good English papers, which soon were recognized and printed in the *Helios*, the school paper. After I had come to know him better, I found his one secret longing was to be "a newspaper man" but he was sure that was impossible because of the constant need for selling papers which he was sure could lead nowhere. His only idle minutes came when he fell asleep in class.

Many helpful plans were worked out to help this unusual and ambitious, but bitter boy. On the day he graduated, he started his first assignment with *The Evening Press*, as a newspaper man.

A year later I received a letter from the manager, expressing his pleasure over Cornelius' work and that he was directly in line for promotion. Recently I have heard from him. He holds a prominent official position in Grand Rapids.

One of my students at Central High School was Stewart Edward White, who has since delighted us with his many, many books of adventure.

He entered high school in 1888 as a second-year student. This was not only his first day at Central but his first day in any school. He had been reared in a home of wealth but never sank to luxurious idleness. With no need to labor, he has always been a hard worker.

He had escaped the mechanical grind of schools because of private tutors, but he had received a rigid mental discipline. He had read much and intelligently, had traveled extensively and had been allowed to indulge and to cultivate his natural love of outdoor life. He had dreamed and lived the dreams of youth, by streams and lakes and forests and mountains.

He was a good student, but had a manner of seeming indifference. He never volunteered to recite, but when called upon was ready with a well-thought-out answer. He did not aim to be a brilliant student just for the sake of leading, yet few ever out-

Grand Rapids Central High School under Construction (c. 1895)

distanced him.

In those days athletics did not hold the center of stage, and in this particular school were almost unknown. He did much to arouse interest in competitive athletics and was a moving spirit in arranging for the first important field day contest. There was no athletic director, no trainer, nor teacher to assist or advise, so he became his own trainer, and a strict one. He improvised a track in his grandfather's grounds and whatever was considered the proper distance to run each day was run without regard to inclination or weather. This faithful training won him the race. His time would not hold for him any interscholastic record today, but he did it easily and without exhaustion.

Stewart White wrote well in those days, better than most of his class, and more than the others, for he loved to use his pen for his own pleasure. Naturally his books have given me especial pleasure and I still see the boy behind the words as I read.

The old high school building outgrew its quarters and for three years was overcrowded, but we were able to put up with the inconveniences cheerfully for we could finally see a new building growing just down the hill. One February we moved in.

It was a beautiful building, with wide corridors and easy stairways—large recitation rooms although I thought none were as attractive as my old tower room in the old school. The room that was to be mine was an irregular one. Since the building was set against a hill the windows all along that side were something like three feet from the floor. A wide ledge ran all along under the windows. In the corner the foundation walls projected out into the room for perhaps two feet. These irregularities that at first seemed like deformities turned out to be adornments. The projection coming in front of a large window made, when piled with red pillows a fine window seat and furnished a bit of bright color. The wisdom of furnishing such attractive projectiles was questionable but no serious trouble resulted. No doubt the pillows made some flying trips about the room but I never caught them. This corner was a pleasant change from my desk and many an informal talk with a boy or girl was held there.

The long and wide ledge at the back made the right place for ferns and other plants that needed little sun and was a good place for a large bowl of goldfish. In the south windows were geraniums and other blossoming plants. On the wall were a few good pictures, and the corner bookshelves were filled with interesting books.

In administration I tried to produce the feeling that this room was our home for most of the hours of the day and that there must be complete cooperation if we made a success of it. The teacher was not infallible, and she demanded recognition as a human being likely to make mistakes and claiming the same consideration that she tried to give the young people. Her judgement would not always be right, her strength not always equal to every emergency, but she would earnestly try to deal with them, be sympathetic and try to see their side of every question.

During the seven years in charge of this room, this was my attitude as nearly as I can analyze it: School is more than a preparation for life; it is part of life and we have no more right to assume that a young person begins to live only when his school days are over than that the life of a plant begins when it first bursts into bloom. These young days should have in them a sense of obligation and personal responsibility but also a generous touch of life's happiness. All relations should be natural, not artificial. The individual is greater than a system, and any system is false that does not help the individual to expand according to his nature.

Courtesy should be a keynote in student-teacher relationship.

One thing which I have particularly disliked was anything approaching "schoolroom" manners. The social usages that dominate the best society belong equally in the schoolroom. This insistence on courtesy at all times must have made some impression. Soon after moving into our new building, we held open house for the public. Each teacher was in his room, while boys from the senior class were stationed through the corridors and at the doors to direct the guests and announce the name and specialty of each teacher. Late in the evening a friend said to me, "Do you know what the boy at your door is saying? He is telling everyone that this is Mrs. Milner's room and that she teaches mathematics and manners."

Never but once did I give, as I remember, any definite statement as to manners. Mr. Greeson's secretary was a young Hollander who was working his way through school. When he was graduated he was to go to Washington as secretary to one of our Michigan senators, William Alden Smith. Before leaving he said to me, "You know that a person with my background has little chance to know anything about social matters. In Washington I shall have to go about more or less with the senator. Do you know of some book that will keep me from making too serious blunders?"

My answer was much the same that Miss McClellan had given me when I was a young teacher in Niles: "You don't need a book. Keep your eyes open and when in doubt do the commonsense and kindly thing. You cannot thus go far astray."

He told me later that the plan worked to the extent at least of not making the senator ashamed of him. Nowadays self-government is quite an accepted part of many of our schools. In these days I am writing about, 1886-1898, the idea was quite revolutionary. I myself was not persuaded that a whole school could be run properly under student control, but I did believe that as much responsibility should be put upon the students as possible. Frequently my duties as preceptress called me out of the room. When school was in session the boys and girls had become accustomed to my absence for longer or shorter periods, and everything went on as if I were there. Then it occurred to me that it shouldn't be necessary for me to be there in my room to ring a bell to tell high school seniors that it was time for the afternoon session to come to order. I decided to experiment. Mr.

Greeson was sceptical but told me to go ahead. I talked to the class and asked them to assume the responsibility for the beginning of the session without a sound from my desk if I were unavoidably detained. Taking the roll had long been in their hands.

The plan wobbled some at first but soon was going well even under a sudden and severe test that had me worried for a few minutes, when an eminent superintendent from out of town was with Mr. Greeson and me as we made a late entry into the school. He was impressed with the order but remarked, "This is the first *negligee* school I've ever seen."

Edith and Charles, two seniors, were a pair of youthful lovers. Their devotion was an open secret in the school; everybody accepted the situation and the two were always dignified in their relations to each other.

One glorious afternoon in the Spring, they were both absent from school. The logical conclusion was easy to reach.

"Absence or tardiness is to be reported immediately upon entrance to the room," was one of my invariable and oft-repeated rules, so when Edith came the next morning she applied for the excuse that would admit her to classes.

"My uncle telephoned asking me to take luncheon with him and my aunt downtown yesterday and when we were through it was so late that my aunt said I might stay with her and not come back to school," was the explanation she gave.

I knew the aunt with whom she lived and that was not the sort of thing she was likely to do. I had never known Edith to be anything but truthful, nevertheless I was suspicious. Circumstances on one side and the word of an honest girl on the other left my mind wavering. Unconsciously, I had been looking her steadily in the eye while trying to come to a decision. Her eyes fell and that crystallized my decision. Reaching for my little block of paper, I wrote a full excuse for her absence.

Within a minute, Charles entered the room. His home was not in the city, but in a village some twenty miles away. He gave an equally frail excuse. As with Edith, I looked him squarely in the eye as I gave him his permit without question.

In a leisure period in the afternoon, Charles sat down beside me. "Edith says I must tell you that we both lied this morning. She says that you didn't believe us. We went for a drive. She wanted to tell you the truth but she had promised me not to. It was all my fault so please give me all the punishment."

"Well, tell me about it."

"She didn't go to luncheon with the aunt. It was such a beautiful afternoon that I teased her to go for a drive. She didn't want to go at all, for she said you would find it out, or that she would have to tell you."

"Did you have a happy time?"

"A happy time? I should say not. Edith was as glum as could be, and couldn't think of anything except that she had run away from school."

"And you?"

"Boys don't care about things as girls do. But I didn't like to see Edith feel so bad."

"But why did you think you needed to lie about it to me? Do you think that because my hair is gray that I cannot understand how strongly, on a Summer day like yesterday, the open country calls to young people who care for each other?"

"Would you have let us go if we had asked?"

"Perhaps I might have remembered by own youth," I replied half to myself.

"Mrs. Milner, will you forgive us and punish me? It was all my fault. I planned it and made Edith promise to lie to you. Please don't punish her."

"Edith has had her punishment already. As for you, let me say that when a young man has so won the regard of a girl that she will lie at his direction, he has gained a power that it behooves him to use for good rather than evil."

Charles looked in amazement at a teacher who could be content to leave him with the burden of his own wrongdoing. I think he realized that his action had swept beyond the question of school discipline to a life lesson.

The second year in the new building was the year that I became preceptress with many new responsibilities. It was also at this time that my husband was taken desperately ill with an attack of typhoid fever. For weeks his life hung in the balance with little hope for his recovery. It is not necessary to describe the anxious days when I went back and forth between school and sickroom, often walking the distance several times a day and for some weeks finding it necessary to abandon school entirely. Let it suffice to say that my husband recovered very slowly and for all the rest of his short life was a semi-invalid.

During the summer of 1897 my husband and Mr. Greeson went on a sailing trip into the Lake Superior region in search of fish and health. I spent the summer in Ann Arbor.

Frederick L. Bliss, for some years principal of Detroit Central High School, had, the preceding year, left the public schools and with Harry G. Sherrard established a private preparatory school for boys which was called Detroit University School. In the spring of 1897 Mr. Bliss had visited the Grand Rapids Central High School and had spent most of the time in my room. I had thought nothing of it at the time, for we had many visitors and my room being the gathering place for the seniors, it was naturally a point of interest. I only thought that Mr. Bliss and I agreed pretty thoroughly on most matters concerning schools.

In July he came to Ann Arbor to see me. He told me much about the school in Detroit, its plans, its prospects, its needs. It had started with enthusiasm and everything pointed to its success. He was looking for someone to put in charge of the secondary department and wanted me to take that position. Although the salary was not much greater than my present one, the opportunities and prospects were alluring. But my husband's practice had been good before his illness and naturally his profession must come first, so I declined the offer.

My husband returned from this fishing trip with improved health, and life looked good indeed as we started on a new school year. He resumed his practice for all that year, but found it greatly interrupted by recurring illnesses and his strength at no time quite equal to the demands upon it. The long illness with its attendant heavy expenses, and the interrupted medical practice and retarded convalescence, made some plans for increased salary necessary.

Those years were difficult ones for married teachers, public opinion demanding that a wife should not work, so the school board had many problems to face. The president of the board made it very clear that I was a problem as he said one day, "Mrs. Milner, if it were not for you, we would have to fire all married teachers."

"What do you want me to do, resign or get a divorce?" was my retort. "We know that you won't get a divorce and the board won't let you go, so you see what a predicament we are in."

A small increase was granted, and in spite of a greatly increased offer from Detroit there was every hope that my husband's health would improve and that what had been lost could be recovered. So it was best to accept the compromise and try to reconcile myself to what the board evidently considered a generous increase.

Within a short time, however, another illness struck, and another offer from Detroit arrived offering nearly a fifty percent increase, so a grave decision must be made. I went to the physician who had taken care of my husband during this long siege and stated the necessity for knowing the truth as to my husband's health. He hesitated but finally replied that he and his brother had consulted on the case very carefully and felt compelled to tell me that there was very little prospect of his ever being able to carry on a full practice again. They felt that he might live for several years and be able to look after a limited number of patients but that he would not likely ever to be strong again.

It seemed as though I must take the offer that would give us the adequate and necessary support which my present salary did not make possible, but how could this be done without discouraging my husband or hurting his pride? A solution to this problem came from Detroit, in the form of letters from many of his former patients now living there, who had often before written expressing the wish that he were there. Now, having heard of Mr. Bliss's offer to me, they wrote again, urging us to come, setting forth the advantages of living in Detroit and assuring him that the nucleus of a practice was awaiting him. While we never discussed the matter, I am sure that with his medical knowledge he realized the precarious condition of his health and hoped that the lightened work might in time lead to full recovery. At any rate, without visible wrench the decision was made, and I sent in my resignation to take effect at the end of the term.

"Preceptress Florence Milner Receives Flattering Offer."

"The chances are that Grand Rapids will lose Mrs. Florence Milner of the Central School, one of the most capable and best liked teachers in the city and state. Mrs. Milner is wanted in Detroit and Mr. Bliss of the University School is determined to have her. The offers are so flattering that it does not seem possible that Grand Rapids will be able to off-set them.

Offer after offer has been made for the past year and Mr. Bliss still holds the place for her. He has offered 60 per-

cent over what she is now receiving.

It is desired that she take a part in shaping the policy of the new school. All over the state it is known what a power Mrs. Milner has been in determining the policy of the Grand Rapids school. Lately and since she has been Preceptress, it has been part of her duties to shape, with the principal, the course of study in school, and in that capacity she has won the esteem of the teachers and pupils of her own school and has acquired a state reputation of no mean degree.

Probably no teacher who has ever been in the high school has been a closer friend to boys who did not like to work, who wanted to drop their studies, and who were mainly interested in fun. It is true, too, that of these sort of boys she has made more good men and put more fellows on the right road than has any other teacher."

From a clipping in the *Grand Rapids Press*

The question of the employment of married teachers in the public schools becomes, at intervals, the storm center in their administration. Forty-four years of teaching in both public and private schools, twenty-three of them as a married teacher, should give me the right, both from experience and observation, to speak with a modicum of authority on the subject.

As mentioned above, the matter arose during my years in Grand Rapids. In my later years there, a strong effort was made to displace all married teachers. I was then preceptress of the Central High School, head of the department of Mathematics, and in charge of the senior study room. The discussion was fast and furious. As one of the bones of contention, I did not feel called upon to enter the struggle, but trusted my record and merely insisted that, if the Board knew anyone who could fill the position better, its duty to the city demanded that they replace me by that better teacher. I could not see why being married per se had any bearing on the case. The argument repeatedly brought forward was that, with a husband to take care of me, I had no right to hold the place from a young woman who had to earn her own living.

At that time, I thought it unwise to say anything about the salary, governed in this decision as much by consideration of the other married teachers as for myself, but it hurt my pride not to have the service which the Board admitted was more than satisfactory given proper recognition. In school I could forget the slight but I was always conscious of it when at the end of the month the inadequate check was handed to me. Then my blood boiled at the seeming injustice and each month my temperature rose a little higher.

The whole question, it seems to me, has been argued from the wrong standpoint. Then, as now, the answer is that the schools are not semi-charitable institutions: the business of a School Board is not finding jobs for the unemployed. The position should go, by rights, to the one who can, in its judgment, do the work best. It should never ask the question whether a teacher is rich or poor, married or single. If one has in her great teaching ability, if she can hold as in the hollow of her hand a school and do with it as she will, if she can lead her young people through experiences that will toughen their moral fiber, if she can do all these things, a city or town should do all in their power to keep her in their service. Great teachers are too rare for any community to be willing to pare one of them. There are hordes — I almost said "herds" — of indifferent teachers, armies of fairly good ones but only now and then is there one with the wisdom of Arnold or the real spirit of the Great Teacher. When such a one is found, every possible inducement should be put forth to keep that teacher in the school instead of raising barriers against her.

Do not mistake me as arguing in favor of married teachers against single ones. I am only arguing, and I wish I might do it with unction, in favor of the best teachers be they married or single. Occasionally, even now, the campaign against married teachers breaks out somewhere; although, with women now filling every sort of position, the agitation is less frequent, and some day, let us hope, will die away entirely.

The Detroit University School

I n starting the story of the sixteen years spent in the Detroit University School (1900-1916), perhaps a few paragraphs from a letter I sent to *The Helios*, a publication of the Grand Rapids High School students, will best describe what I found.

November 15, 1900

Dear Helios:

When I left Grand Rapids it was with the promise to tell you something about my new school as soon as I felt at home in it. This condition was reached the first day, but I have waited to know more of the details of the institution and to decide what would most interest you.

Detroit University School is a private school exclusively for boys. Mr. Bliss, for years the principal of the Detroit Central High School, was the originator and is its principal. Mr. H.G. Sherrard, who was also long in the high school at the head of the department of Greek and Latin, is associate principal.

The school is temporarily in the quarters of the Michigan Athletic Association, which, with surprising ingenuity, has been adapted to school use. The building stands upon one corner of the four acre lot, and bears little resemblance to the conventional school house. The reception hall has been converted into a library, and partitions have been thrown up in varying lines to mark off recitation rooms on the first floor. The second floor is taken up by the study room for the intermediate department, its recitation rooms, and the

85

well-equipped gymnasium. Connected with this building, and running along close to the street, was the old grandstand. This has also been transformed, and here is my own room, the study hall for the secondary department. By necessity of its original use, it is a long narrow room, and accommodates, in close quarters, the ninety boys in the grades corresponding to the high school. Beyond this, is the room where I have my few recitations, and still beyond, the clay modeling and art room. In the story below are the shops and laboratories, while overhead is the first primary room, the large luncheon room and the kitchen.

Our noon intermission is only forty minutes, and few are near enough to go home for luncheon. The dining room accommodates the school and a good hot luncheon is served each day.

But this is merely the shell; the real school is the boys. Only a year ago it opened its doors, and today it has an enrollment of two hundred. It begins with the first year of primary work and prepares for all the good colleges and universities, including Harvard and Yale, and its diploma is accepted by such as admit without examination. Of the thirteen boys who were graduated last June, ten are now in college. The present class numbers sixteen, all of whom are definitely planning to enter college next fall.

The curriculum does not differ materially from that of our best high schools. In the size of the classes, however, there is a marked difference, as it is the policy of the school that no class shall exceed twenty, and very few reach that number. It is really possible to teach geometry to sections of sixteen.

The manual training is an important and interesting feature. Mr. Skinner, who made the reputation of the Toledo schools in that direction, is in full charge of the work here. The course is carefully graded and includes mechanical drawing, shopwork, clay modeling, and free-hand drawing. Each boy has two periods a day set apart for this branch, and they find it a pleasure to devote their spare time to it in addition.

You will be especially interested in the encouragement given to athletics. The building does not take up much of the four acres, and the rest of the space is a fine athletic field.

At one side are two excellent tennis courts. Then there is a good running track one-sixth of a mile in length, football and baseball fields in season and room beside for various games. From my seat in the "grandstand" it is not unusual to look out upon tennis, football practice, skittles, shinney, quoits, and tether-ball all in full swing at the same time. The last period in the afternoon all members of the two football teams not in recitation are out for practice. When the play is over, they return to the basement of the building, where each boy has his own locker, and where there are fine showers. In addition to the coach, there is a physical director who makes a careful examination of each boy and directs his work in the gymnasium.

One exceedingly interesting feature of the school is the home department, and it is exactly what its name indicates — a real home for boys from out of town. Mr. and Mrs. Skinner, who have charge of the department, have solved the problem of taking these boys actually into their family and of giving them the same supervision and consideration that they bestow upon their own children. The house is at present filled to its utmost capacity, but there is a waiting list and something will be done at Christmas time to make room for a few more. It is the purpose, however, to retain always the home spirit and the home freedom, let the numbers be what they may, and with the right people in charge this will be easily possible.

Above everything else the school proposes to stand for good scholarship, at the same time giving boys a happy, wholesome life under friendly supervision. The school certainly has a future and the boys who find it possible to come here are fortunate indeed.

As to myself, I am very happy in my work and feel that "the lines are fallen unto me in pleasant places."

When I stepped into that room where I was to spend sixteen years, searching eyes fairly bored holes into me. As I studied the boys that day, they seemed but little different from those in Grand Rapids. As a whole they were uniformly better dressed and there was a little more of ease of manner, greater familiarity with what is termed good form. Their faces were the same faces of boys eager for life, full of physical energy, ready to meet half way anyone who would play the game according to the rules. From that first hour I was grateful for the opportunity to work with these boys and realized that my contact with them must be direct and simple.

Mr. Bliss was a man of large experience in educational work and in human nature as well. He knew boys — their needs, their ambitions, their faults, their joys, and, best of all, their sorrows. He understood that the sorrows of youth are not the trifles that so many older people consider them. The boys called him "the Bear," and whoever knows the habits of young people can see in the title the proof of the high regard in which he was held. The origin of the name rested somewhere back in the early days of the school. No one knew just how it came about and each new boy wondered whether this title came from the severe, sometimes almost savage expression that his face assumed in serious moments or from the immense white polar bear skin that covered the center of the office floor. At any rate, to the boys, he was the Bear and the office, the Bear's Den.

The Bear had decided that the influence of a woman, in some place of real importance where she could be brought natually into close relationship with the boys, would be of great value. So, contrary to every precedent at that time, he had decided to place me in charge of the study room where one hundred and fifty boys of the high school grades spent all of their time when not in recitation.

Detroit University School, Elmwood at Larned (1900)

Although most of the boys were sons of the well- to-do and the wealthy, the Bear had consciously and persistently worked to bring in boys from various conditions of life. His keen sense of the value of the democratic spirit convinced him that the only way to keep that spirit was to make membership democratic. The result was a very interesting study of boys and their reaction to each other and to the school. I was fascinated with the way each newcomer was studied with amazing keenness of vision by the old boys. The normal, whole-souled boy didn't care whether the new boy was the son of a millionaire mineowner from Montana or was paying his way by helping about the dormitory, cleaning windows, or shoveling snow. The only point considered was the kind of stuff in him. If the new boy was true to himself, alive, ready for fun, enthusiastic, and to be depended upon, he won the confidence of his associates rather easily. This confidence was never expressed in words but manifested itself in a thousand little ways. To show that he even existed was one proof, for the boys never wasted time on meaningless courtesies to the unfavored. A vigorous punch in passing, a wrestling bout that would terrify the uninitiated, the bestowing of a nickname, were some of the ways boys then (and now) showed their regard for each other.

Several times another type of boy made his appearance. Sometimes the fault was snobbery or egotism, or cowardice or affectation, or the lack of courtesy or consideration, bad manners at table or about the dormitory. It took a surprisingly short time for the old boys to discover these qualities. Someone once said, "There is an animal in creation of no general merit, but it has the eye of a hawk for affectation. It is called a boy." The saying is definitely true. When this type of boy arrived, one of two things always happened: either little by little the fellows and the school made a man of him, or failing of that, he was left so completely to himself that his stay was usually limited.

Almost always, however, the first happened. Several instances come to mind and although the cure was sometimes difficult and the patient perverse, most boys are innately desirous of winning the approbation of their peers, and so were these boys. What real pleasure I felt when gradually I could see such a boy win his spurs, and become a member of the family, and acquire a nickname.

The matter of nicknames became quite a matter of study on my part and since I was writing a series of articles for the *Detroit*

Saturday Night and other periodicals at this time, I wrote one on this subject. Nicknames are sometimes so far-fetched that a knowledge of their evolution is necessary to account for their eccentricity. Campbell, if you pronounce it in the true Scotch fashion, fairly begs for "Dromedary" which may shorten to "Drom" or even "Hump." When the father is an officer in the National Bisquit Company his son could not be anything but "Crackers." When a boy's first name is Milo, naturally he is dubbed "Venus."

Sometimes the rule of contraries was called into play. "Tanner" had an enormous appetite. "Sliver" weighed two hundred pounds. "Cupid" was actually heavy and never known to move quickly. "Chatter" never spoke if he could make a smile do. Somewhere Lewis Carroll explains that many of the words in "Jaberwocky" are the result of attempting to speak two or more words at the same time, as when slim and lithe become slithy. By a similar trick, Harry Fletcher evolved into "Heffles," Wallace Osborn into "Wazzy" and Charles Kanter into "Kax." "Pinky" and "Chick" were athletic stars, and so the list could go on and on. Every school could furnish a long and interesting list of ingenious nicknames, I am sure. Besides the ones mentioned are some others, all from the Detroit University School: "Fish," "Snipe," "Piggy," "Skin," "Bubbles," "Ham," "Bounce," "Swifty," "Spider," "Squibs." All belong to Detroit. You will find many of them transacting business today, but under different names!

For the first few years in Detroit we had our own apartment and my mother lived with us. My husband's office was downtown and my school not far away.

After Dr. Milner's death I moved into the school and had an apartment there, in the dormitory. Although I had no responsibility for the boys, my rooms opened into the large living room often occupied by the boys in the evenings and weekends for games and reading. I therefore spent a good deal of time with them, visiting before the open fire. Here was a priceless experience in getting to know the boys, their problems, and their ideals. Sometimes, I would invite a few into my apartment for a chafing dish supper on a Sunday evening, and many were the heated discussions that occurred there. Here all sorts of interests were talked over and plans made for the future as well as the strategy for the next football game.

Athletics had not held as prominent place in the schools then

Florence Milner and "her boys" at the Detroit University School

as they do now. At the D. U. S. they were recognized as a means, not only of spirited contests but as a necessary agency for the building up of the physical part of every boy in the school. This had many times been neglected in their home life.

One of the great delights of my life at D. U. S. was the daily contact with all sports. Every track meet, every baseball and football game found me on the grandstand or sidelines. Our field was in full view of my windows and furnished me with pleasant diversion during the day, when the younger boys were at their prescribed athletics. Frequently I spent much time after school watching practice and the various tryouts for track and field. The boys were surprised to find a woman with a genuine and reasonably intelligent interest in all their sports. It was not long before they accepted it as a matter of course and used to talk with me about what was to most of the school a vital matter.

Before this, my knowledge had been somewhat general. Now I began to pay attention to details. The boys, finding me really anxious for information, gave it in abundance. Soon I knew every interscholastic record on track and field and watched our own boys with respect to such records. I sat by "Pinky" when he rose to clear the bar in the high jump of six feet, establishing a new interscholastic record, and eventually sending him to the Olympic Games. I even felt that I had a share in his achievement for I held his half-sucked lemon when he went out to try for that record.

It was in connection with athletics that the boys bestowed upon me a mark of confidence of which I have been very proud. They say that I asked intelligent questions about certain of the football plays and was able to grasp them when explained and diagrammed. The members of the team never tired of instructing me and I never tired of learning. One night the captain and manager of the team came to me in a mysterious manner and asked for a private interview. They took me into a recitation room, closed the door, and then opened it once or twice to make sure that no eavesdroppers were about and then proceeded with their mission.

They had decided to give me the team's signals, for they thought it would add greatly to my enjoyment of the games if I knew them. I was overwhelmed by this unusual mark of confidence and am still proud of it today. But when I looked at their diagrams it seemed to me that I could never master them. No problem in geometry, algebra, or trigonometry ever looked so complicated. I could not fall down on them so I tackled them, one at a time, working as I had in my early tangles with problems. The boys helped me and put me through vigorous drill until I began to see the light. By watching practice after school, I eventually understood most of them and gained some quickness in visualizing the plays before they started. The boys on the team delighted in rattling off a signal as they passed my desk, expecting me to call the play, and sometimes I was able to do it. From that time on, my interest in and enjoyment of football have become fixed.

As anyone can see, the D. U. S. was an unusual school. We were able to have rules and break them occasionally, with no bad results, just as families are able to make "special rules" for certain times. The circus parade was one of these. Who can resist a circus parade, but alas — they are no more. Our school was but one short block from Jefferson Avenue, down which all parades passed. It became an unwritten law that at the first sound of band or calliope, it should be taken for a general signal. Whether in study or recitation room, shop, or art, or in the field, every boy was at liberty to start at once without waiting for permission. I remember the amazement on the face of a new teacher who knew nothing of the custom, when his class suddenly rose and rushed from the room without ceremony. The teachers always followed along but not quite so speedily.

By the time the head of the parade reached Elmwood Avenue, the entire school was lined up on either side of Jefferson. It was an amusing crowd. Some boys had unconsciously brought their books along or a catcher's mitt or ball, while one boy was seen clutching a hammer he had been using in shop. A snap shot is extant of such a line with myself grasping an ice cream soda which one of the boys had brought me from Bert's, a valuable adjunct to the school. All were intent on watching the elephants as they paraded down the avenue.

Out of a perfectly natural impulse there grew a custom which was observed each year as long as I remained in the school. It was one of those glorious mornings in May when

"Skies are clear and grass in growing/The breeze comes whispering in our ears/That dandelions are blossoming near."

And so they were, all over the field, glittering like gold. Standing at the window I watched the boys gathering them. One boy brought me a bunch of long-stemmed ones which I put at my belt. This gave me an idea. When the bell rang for assembly, I stood at the door and stationed a boy at the other, each of us with a handful of dandelions. Each boy, as he entered, was given one and asked to wear it. At the opening exercises I said a few words about the beauty of the morning and then read Lowell's "The Dandelions."

The next year, with the appearance of the yellow flowers, one of the boys asked, " When is Dandelion Day?"

"Dandelion Day?" I could not think of what he meant.

"Don't you remember the day we brought you dandelions and we all wore one and you read us a poem about them."

"Yes, but I didn't know you had given the day a name."

"We've always called it 'Dandelion Day.' Can't we have a program and decorate the room and make it real — well, you know the kind of thing I mean."

Of course, I agreed and appointed a flower committee and program committee and assured them that I would be glad to help as needed. The lower school, including the primary and kindergarten, were invited to join.

No morning could be more glorious than that Fifteenth of May. Bookcases and window ledges were banked with flowers. There were lilacs, purple and white, dogwood, and other flowering shrubs that made background for the more delicate flowers. One high window was banked with green and starred with dandelions. Under this in large letters formed of dandelions was "Dandelion Day."

Each year the program varied. This second observance, one of the boys told the story of the first day and said that it was the hope of the school that the custom would continue. "We have called it 'Dandelion Day' but that has become only a symbol for a general flower day." And that is how it was afterwards celebrated.

Once a student wrote a paper about banquet garland, the wreaths of bay and laurel, and the palm of victory of the Greeks and Romans. At another time, there was an account of the flowers of the Bible, and another year those of Shakespeare. Someone suggested a contest in which each would write, in a given time, the names of as many flowers as he could remember and record withing the time limit. There was music on the ukulele with the player wearing a Hawaiian lei made of soft green and dandelions. There were recitations about flowers, many of those by the younger boys. It was surprising how many poems we found when be began to hunt for them.

The youth of today no longer "speak pieces" and do little committing to memory of selections of any length, but those trained in the old tradition have a valuable storehouse of literature.

The annual picnic was one of the things looked forward to even from the first days in the fall. The old boys talked about it constantly and the new boys soon caught the fever. Everybody who lived in the dormitory planned to give up all else on that day, and from the time the day was set, the home boys were the envy of the town boys who could not go.

The housekeeper was a regular fairy godmother when it came to preparing the luncheon, and the mysterious baskets could well be taken by faith and on the pledge of former years when the supply of good things which they contained were still a subject of tender recollection.

Mr. Skinner was nothing short of a general in the way he marshaled his forces, assigned tasks and responsibilities, and finally got the people all together at the dock just at the end of Belle Isle Bridge. A few of the boys were to walk across the bridge to the Boat Club and, getting small canoes, were to paddle through the canals and lagoons up to the head of Belle Isle, where supper was to be served. For the others two large war canoes were waiting at the dock. Mr. Skinner took charge of one, giving the other over to Peter Pat, who was as much at home on water as on land.

Mrs. Skinner and I were assigned seats in different boats, while two of the smallest boys were allowed to curl up in the bottom of each canoe. The rows of paddles on each side were taken possession of by the big boys and the two big canoes swung out into the great river.

Both canoes headed straight to the opening into the canals half way up the island, finding a path among the sail boats, yachts and launches that were thick on this side of the island. Both captains urged the men to greatest exertion at the paddles, for it was always a contest to see who could enter the entrance first. The charm of the spot never failed to touch everyone to silence; only the lap of the paddles broke the stillness as the boats moved under the overarching trees and across mirrored lagoons. The wooded silence bore the hush of a real forest, which a wise city had left untouched by any artificial gardening. It was the perfect playground of a fortunate city.

At the head of the island the canoe swept out of the canals heading up toward Lake St. Clair, which spread and shimmered to the north. A few strokes of the paddle brought the crafts around the point to the little landing where those who had come in the smaller skiffs were already waiting. They had set up the red and blue flag bearing the letters D.U.S. at the end of the pier, and the school colors waved from each canoe.

Supper was always the first business. One long table was selected and the boys were willing helpers, especially when it came to sampling the various baskets. Mr. Skinner had his own clever way of making coffee and taught the boys much practical woodcraft. A ravenous crowd gathered around the table where fried chicken, sandwiches of a half dozen varieties, potato salad, cold meats, eggs, cookies, and cakes jostled each other in profusion.

At first silence reigned, but the first edge of their appetites being satisfied tongues were loosed and the meal a merry one, and always the miracle was reinacted of the stowing away of a fabulous amount of edibles.

After supper there were always games in which the men joined with the boys and there was the usual amazement on the part of young people that there was anything like fun, real fun, in older people.

Later the party would break up into groups, some going for a walk in the woods, others paddling along the shore in the small canoes. Many would be finally attracted by the gorgeous sunset and gather on the western bank to watch its full glory. Here conversation would take a surprising turn — the adults leading at first. The intense beauty of the hour brought a natural response in thoughts of art, of painting, of music, of opera, of books, of high experiences of the past, and dreams for the future, although one night in 1910 when we had all been keenly interested in the sight of Halley's Comet, the present loomed high as we marveled at the heavens and the whole world of astronomy. Many were the responses of some boy who perhaps for the first time in his life realized something of his own potential for feeling. One such boy, after our discussion of the beauty of the scene, exclaimed in almost a hushed voice, "then, there are some things that don't belong to anyone, like this sunset. No one owns the clouds or the color in them except the people who have seen it here tonight as we have. I feel as though this particular sunset was my very own. Anyhow, no one can take away from me the picture of it."

For the trip home, Mr. Skinner would give them a choice of the two routes back. Always the choice would be for "outside." The canoes would then head up toward the lake to make a wide sweep to avoid the sandbar. They would give the lighthouse a wide berth and then strike out into the broad sweeping Detroit River, a river without equal in all the wide world.

On one side were the long wooded stretches of the island, deep in shadows. On the other shone the low lights of the Canadian shore, while ahead blazed and flashed the brilliant illumination of the city.

Down the watery highway we would see the great ore boats, gliding, the smoke pluming back from their stacks, the lights gleaming from their masts, but silent as phantom ships that ride the waters without a master. The ferry boats would speed back and forth across the river, rocking the canoes in their waves. The stars and the moon made a track of beauty for the canoes carrying their burdens of boys each of whom must have taken back from the long hours in the open a little gain in those higher things which are necessary to round out a boy's nature to the full and noble stature of a man.

I have watched hundreds of high school pupils find their places in the world. Their achievements have run the gamut, all the way from men like Edsel Ford to those who landed on the wrong side of prison doors. Some, from a worldly point of view, have accomplished more than their school life and home conditions promised, some less, but in character so far as I have been able to follow individuals, they have developed into exactly the same type of men that they were boys during the later years of high school. Direction is pretty well determined by this time. President James B. Angell of the University of Michigan evidently held this same position, for he used to say, "I never knew a boy to go wrong in college who didn't have a good running start before he came."

Since the name of Edsel Ford is so well known throughout the world and since I have been asked so many times what kind of boy he was in school days, perhaps a few recollections would be interesting and revealing as to the training he received.

Edsel was always modest. In those days the Ford Motor Company was far from what it is now, although Henry Ford was rapidly becoming a rich man. Edsel had the absolute confidence of his schoolmates. If some activity required dependable executive ability, the verdict often was, "Give it to Ford." If he assumed the responsibility, the boys never gave the matter an anxious thought.

He did his school work in the same definite manner. Whatever the lesson assignment, he met it as an obligation. If anything interfered with his study time, he had the habit of making explanation in advance of class. If he had to be absent, there was always a courteous note from his mother.

He was interested in athletics although he never became a star. He took his place with the rank and file and did whatever was required of him for the good of the team. His special interest was track, where he ran the mile. During training season, at just such a time of day, Edsel could be seen faithfully circling the track as many times as the coach had directed. So far as I remember, he never broke any records, but every meet found him ready to help the team push up the number of points scored, and it is the total number of points that count.

Edsel Ford (far right), Detroit University School Track Team. Unfortunately the others are unidentified.

Our team won one important interscholastic meet by just half a point.

Henry Ford never was in sympathy with the hard and fast system of the then rather closely standardized education. His association with the working man led him to believe in a teaching fitted to the probable future of the individual. He later developed these ideas successfully in the school operated in connection with the Ford plant found and placed in the charge of Mr. F.E. Searle, a man I knew well. Naturally, Edsel, being an only son, was destined to become a part of the then rapidly growing business now expanded to a vastness not dreamed in those days. His father felt that his son would need some things more than a further study of formal courses offered in a college curriculum. In harmony with this idea, at what corresponds to the end of the third year of high school, Edsel left to prepare for his future through travel, through hours in the factory, and in close association with such men as his father, Thomas Edison, Harvey Firestone, and others of similar caliber. Thus was gained his training for the presidency of the Ford Motor Company.

While the plant was still at Highland Park, Edsel took me on one of his regular rounds. We walked for two hours. I was impressed with the fact that his relations with the heads of departments and the men, and his familiarity with every process was the same as his schoolboy attitudes — natural, friendly, modest, intelligent, and efficient.

My acquaintance with Mr. and Mrs. Ford was only incidental, and my knowledge of their home life was such as is reflected in association with the children of any home — in the notes that came from Mrs. Ford and the casual remarks of Edsel concerning his father and mother. One little glimpse, however, of father and son remains. Edsel and I were talking together after school when he suddenly looked at the clock and exclaimed, "I must go. I promised father I'd take him down to Dearborn to see his birds." Mr. Ford had a bird sanctuary even then. This is a rather indefinite picture, but in my imagination I have enjoyed seeing them together. Can't you imagine father and son driving over the road from Detroit to Dearborn, not on the fine highway or in the luxurious car of today but over the old road in a Model T, really a topless, horseless buggy, and then watching the birds and talking about and identifying them? It illustrates an all too rare friendship between a busy executive father and his son.

Edsel married his sweetheart of several years. Eleanor was the belle of their set and Edsel had many rivals. But he knew his own mind and was as unswerving in his attentions as he was to track training. They lived a life of usefulness on their beautiful estate on the shores of Lake St. Clair devoted to their children and giving personal service in many good works.

One afternoon, many years later, in their Grosse Pointe Shores home, I told Edsel and Eleanor and a group from the old school some of the remembrances, when Edsel exclaimed, "Gee, I wish the boys could hear that." It occurred to me that it might be well for other boys to hear the story, not only of Edsel but of others at D.U.S.

In writing about the Model T Ford, I am reminded of an early visit to Detroit in the late eighteen hundreds. There were, I believe, only three pleasure automobiles in Detroit at that time. Harold DuCharme had one and the other two were owned by a large bicycle company. My brother-in-law was their head salesman. One of these cars was a White Steamer. The small engine was in a small open buggy, really just like any other buggy, only with no horse in front. It was steered by a crank or tiller bar like those that persisted in the electrics.

My brother-in-law knew my interest in everything

mechanical and took me for a ride one day. I had watched alertly his handling of the vehicle as we went out Woodward Avenue. We were soon out of heavy traffic, as we called it then, and out into what was real country except for the street cars, which ran way out to Palmer Park. When we had reach- ed the quiet stretch which is now deep in the city, he asked me if I would like to drive. Of course I wanted to and if he thought I could that settled it. He stopped the buggy and we changed seats. He gave me a few directions and told me to go ahead. I had long handled a bicycle and this seemed much the same as to steering, automatic rather than conscious voli- tion. Probably we wobbled more or less but we went ahead with reasonable certainty. Willis said, "Better turn around now," but made no move to change seats. "Oh, you can do it" was his answser to my questioning look. And I did.

When we reached the business section I expected him to displace me but he made no sign other than to say, "I've got to go to the Cadillac so stop there." We were in traffic so I had to be game and drove down Woodward and turned the proper corner and into the porte cocher safely. I wonder if I might not be the first woman to drive a car in Detroit.

Luther and Flora Livingston: The Harvard Connection

T he years in Detroit furnished me with a wealth of fresh experiences and opportunities. The long summers allowed
time for my second love, that of writing, and during the school
years doors were thrown open for conferences and lectures
throughout the state and many parts of the country. In this way
I was privileged to meet and to become a lifelong friend of many
well-known and interesting writers and educators.

Several of my summers were spent at Cape Ann with my husband's sister Flora and her husband, Luther S. Livingston, a
bibliographer of note. Luther and I had been great friends in
Grand Rapids, where he worked in a book store for a time. Flora
had met him on several occasions but she left for Montana about
the time that Luther went to New York, where he was in the rare
book department of Dodd, Mead and Company. On a visit to
Grand Rapids one time, he met with a bicycle accident and was
housebound for some weeks. I visited him often and at my suggestion Flora wrote to him. Eventually the romance blossomed
and they were married in our apartment in Grand Rapids. They
always said that I did their courting for them. Later he was a
member of the firm of Dodd, Livingston and Company and was
responsible for the collection of rare books for many book collectors as well as for libraries, Harvard being among these.

One day I opened a letter from them and out fell two photos,
one a picture of a stretch of ocean shimmering in the sunlight
with a jutting line of jagged rocks against which the water dashed

in snowy spray. The second picture was of a single ship sailing in the moonlight over a hushed sea.

Flora wrote, "Our cottage stands on the rocks two hundred feet from the sea and we look out upon the beauty of which we are sending you a feeble hint. Three sides of *your* room catch the same view. The Poet's corner commands only a part of the scene but there is ocean even from his windows."

"You can't find a "no" in any language that we can understand so we shall meet the six o'clock train and carry you and the Poet to Rockridge."

Luther's letter was equally characteristic. "We can't offer you such a garden as ours at home but here on Cape Cod, Nature is a pretty successful gardener and you shall have flowers. Books we can promise and a hearthstone as a humble substitute for your "Friendly Fire." There will be easy chairs and with you and the Poet, there is sure to be good talk."

We went. Who could resist? What a restful and invigorating spot it was, ever changing in mood and atmosphere and with the horizon ever challenging one's dreams. Here I was able to devote mornings and often the afternoons to my writing. Late afternoons and evenings were spent walking and visiting.

Often, weather permitting, we gravitated to the veranda after dinner, where Flora and the Poet preempted the Gloucester hammock, leaving the steamer chairs to Luther and me. The waves swished gently against the rocks below. A motor boat would fidget around the harbor for a time, but finally, to our relief, it would take its disrupting whir off to other bays.

On cool or rainy evenings, a fire was most welcome. The cheer of the bright flame drew us to the hearth for coziness. The firelight danced the length of the great living room, lighting fitfully the books in their low cases. It brought into sharpness against the soft brown wall the tall blossom-laden stalks of Henry I lilies on the top of the book case, for in this house books and flowers divided the kingdom impartially. The light flitted across the face of the old clock in the corner just to let us know that we had a long evening before us.

On such an evening, Luther would settle comfortably into his Morris chair at one side of the fireplace, Flora in her favorite little rocker at the other side, knitting needles flitting through a ball of soft yarn, the Poet stretched out easily in a chair seemingly made for one of his height, while I gathering into my arms the purring bundle of Blackie Daw and would settle myself with a sigh of anticipation. On such a night I knew, as the occults say, that "conditions were right" for a good talk.

What a wealth of knowledge was in the mind of our rare book collector. He could talk of First Folios, of rare Americana, and of choice autograph letters. He opened a whole new world to me. At one time I had thought books were important only for their reading value, although I had had one encounter that hinted that there were other values. A friend with whom I had enjoyed some absorbing talks on certain schools of philosophy, sent me James Martineau's *Types of Ethical Theory* in two volumes on large paper and well bound. I acknowledged the courtesy, but added that I didn't know just when I would be able to read them.

"Bless you," he wrote back immediately. "I didn't expect you to read the books. I sent them for their static value."

Courtesy: Grand Rapids Public Library Michigan Room

Flora and Luther Livingston (n.d.)

And now I was to discover that books had other values as well. What wondrous tales we heard of rare books and why they were rare, of the many and intricate and mysterious ways of tracing and verifying first editions. Luther even knew how many copies there were of certain valuable books and where they were located. He showed us one evening a very common-looking gray-colored paper board bound book, frayed and papers loose. It was a pamphlet called "New England Prospects" bearing the date 1634. He had two others of the same title but dated some twenty years earlier. He said that these two were probably worth about four hundred dollars but that the later would bring two thousand. The reason was simple. There were numerous pamphlets of the earlier date, but only ten known copies of the 1634 one. He proceeded to tell where each of the ten were located, saying that when a rare book is found, it is necessary not only to know the number of copies but also the condition and location of each one.

After such an evening of hobnobbing with first editions, "one of the few known copies," books in "original boards," "tall copies," and uncut and unopened volumes, my head would be in a whirl. As I stroked Blackie Daw's shining coat and looked into the gleaming coals, I saw awed visions of books valued at thousands and thousands of dollars, of rare manuscripts, and rich bindings, as well as humble ones. My thought of them was reverential. Someday, I thought, I might be able to treat them with careless familiarity of the bibliophile, to handle them as a florist tosses about his roses and his orchids, or as a jeweler lets diamonds and rubies trickle through his fingers upon the pile beneath, but that time has never come. I still feel breathless and awed in the presence of beautiful books.

Almost every man who makes a great success in any one direction has a side line at which he plays. The avocation of Luther S. Livingston was gardening. In his wonderful garden in Scarsdale, New York, there grew every perennial that could be made to live in that climate. His three acres of woodland became a small botanical museum and became a favorite spot for an ever increasing circle of friends on a Sunday afternoon.

In his Michigan home, as a boy, he roamed the open country until it gave up to him the secrets of all its hidden beauty. He learned the Latin names of plants and their peculiarities. Because of this accurate and intense interest, he was sent one year to South America to collect rare orchids and other plants for a famous greenhouse in New Jersey. He later compiled a plant catalogue which became almost a classic for horticulturists. Flora shared his love of plants. She had lived in the Rocky Mountains and knew and loved their unique flora so the two of them spent their holidays and weekends tramping over the hills, greeting the familiar plants, hunting new ones, and carrying them back to the city. They had poppies from California of a rare species and many others from all parts of the country. They knew their flowers as though they were personal friends. The Latin names were at their tongues and they spoke them as naturally as the rest of us poor mortals say dandelion and violet.

Their neighbors, the Walkers, were people of high intelligence, but the familiarity of the Livingstons with every growing thing never ceased to amaze them.

One evening Mr. Walker was reading aloud to his wife when he encountered a strange word.

"What does it mean, Mona?" he asked.

"I don't know," replied his wife, "whether it is the name of a disease or a new flower in the Livingston garden."

These summers spent at Cape Ann, with various trips throughout New England, often including a visit in Cooperstown with Della Thompson Lutes, editor of *American Motherhood* and a personal friend, brought me back to Detroit and my boys with eager anticipation of another year's close associations at D.U.S.

The Farnsworth Room

During Commencement week of 1915, I attended the dedication of the new Harry Elkins Widener Memorial Library at Harvard. This magnificent building was reared by Mrs. George D. Widener of Philadelphia in loving memory of her son, who had lost his life on the *Titanic* in 1912. The young man, only twenty-seven at the time of his death, had graduated from Harvard in 1907 and in those short years had so cultivated and indulged his excellent taste that he had won for himself a place among discriminating collectors of rare books.

Upon graduation, he had sought the advice of Luther as to the collection of books, and their acquaintanceship had ripened into a warm personal friendship. He had always been an avid reader and early in his college course the desire for first editions of the authors he loved, the rarest editions of their kind became an absorbing interest. Later, he demanded even more than this, books that had some personal association. In consequence, his collection became largely what is known as an associational library. He wanted to feel that the hands of the author had touched that particular volume or that his pen had written the inscription bestowing the book upon a friend.

The collection followed the direction of his taste, as it had developed up to that time. It is interesting to wonder what fields it might have traveled had he lived. He was especially fond of Dickens, Thackeray, Tennyson, Browning, and Stevenson. He possessed rare copies of almost everything they ever wrote, besides many manuscripts and personal letters. Wherever he traveled, by train or shipboard, a favorite book was with him, generally one of Stevenson. One man who knew him well says that he had read *Treasure Island* at least thirteen times. This Stevenson collection was for a long time the most complete one ever brought together and perhaps it still is.

Before he started for England, in this tragic year of 1912, he had been planning how he might help raise a fund which eventually would result in an adequate fireproof library building for Harvard, to replace the old Gore Hall. This impressive structure, a loving mother's tribute to a devoted son, is the fulfillment of this wish.

As soon as Mrs. Widener had conceived the idea of the library with a memorial room set aside for her son's personal collection, she had requested that Luther be named the librarian in charge of the room. She said that her son had expressed his greatest admiration, gratitude, and personal fondness for Mr. Livingston hundreds of times, and that if he could ever afford it he would love to have him as his own librarian. Because of Luther's remarkable memory for minute details and his ability to recognize peculiarities in volumes, he had the instinctive confidence of rare book dealers in this country and in London as well, so his appointment was generally considered as the best that possibly could be made.

Widner Library, 1915

By one of the curious and unexplainable twists of life, Luther, who had suffered many difficulties from anemia as a young man, was stricken on the very day of the *Titanic* disaster, and spent many months under the expert care of the doctors at the Rockefeller Institute for Medical Research. On November 30, 1914, the Corporation of Harvard appointed him librarian of the Harry Elkins Widener Memorial Library. One month later, he was buried from Appleton Chapel.

George Parker Winship, who had for twenty years been in charge of the John Carter Brown Library at Providence, was made librarian of the Widener Memorial Room, and Flora, who had gained her knowledge of rare books through seventeen years study with her husband, was made the assistant.

On the desk of the librarian were placed the furnishings that were on the desk of Harry Widener's own room where he dwelt among his books. His medals, mementoes of college association, were also placed in the room. At Mrs. Widener's direction fresh flowers were to be placed there every day. In fact the place was so constructed and dominated by the taste of the loving mother that it was not at all like a part of a vast public structure, but rather the charming private library of a young gentleman. The portrait of the young Widener hanging over the big marble-framed fireplace, the books, the flowers, and furnishings reflected an atmosphere of such realism that it seemed as though Harry Widener still lived among his books.

In August of 1916, I resigned from the Detroit University School. For the first time in my life, I had been seriously ill for some months. This gave me time to face myself and make a few decisions. I decided that this would be a good time to start a new career — and to devote myself to writing.

Just two weeks after making this radical decision, however, an invitation arrived from Harvard asking me to take charge of the new Farnsworth Room that was to be opened in the Widener Library.

This room had long been the dream of the director of the University Library and one of the finest locations had been set aside until such a dream could become a reality. He envisioned a room, beautiful as it could be made, with a small, carefully selected collection of books, among which a student could browse at will — but different from what we now call "browsing rooms." He had the conviction that many students would settle down to read whole books, if they were within easy reach.

Now, through the beneficience and personal interest of Mr. and Mrs. Farnsworth of Dedham and Boston, the director's dream had

Farnsworth Room, 1916

come true. This room was planned as a memorial to their son, Harry Weston Farnsworth of the class of 1912, a young man who had been a journalist with the Providence *Journal* when the war broke out. He enlisted witn the French Foreign Legion. His letters from the front told of the pleasure he was having in reading such books as Pickwick, Plutarch, Lamb, Milton, Shakespeare, Dante, and even *War and Peace*. But he was killed in France September 28, 1915.

The days before I left Detroit, I was overwhelmed by the attentions from my D.U.S. boys, past and present. My rooms were filled with flowers, and notes came in every mail. On the morning of my departure I was escorted to the station by a representative committee of boys, and on my arrival in Boston I was met by a contingent of my boys then at Harvard. Here, too, flowers filled my apartment.

In appearance, the Farnsworth Room was what might be expected in a fine Harvard club. There were comfortable chairs, spacious divan tables with shaded lights, crimson hangings at the windows, walls book- lined to reachable height, with no disfiguring numbers on the books, old portraits, and a mantel with chiming clock, flanked by old Sheffield plate candelabra.

The influence of the Farnsworth Room did not stop with that one unit. So far as is known, at this time only Smith College had a similar room. Its plan, however, was that of a pleasant room for reading or study and relaxation, with no one in charge. It was known as the Browsing Room. We always avoided that name, in the hope that its influence might go a little deeper than nibbling off the buds and sprouts of literature. We felt sure that students, given the opportunity of a good selection of books close by, would find a delight in whole books that would sustain them throughout life, and from letters received throughout the years this did happen. It was to be, both in mental atmosphere and physical equipment, an ideal library for a gentleman. It was distinctive in being the only one known as definitely administered and yet without any suggestion of administration. Students were to have a feeling of perfect freedom. There was only one rule — this room was to be for reading only — or for thinking. No books or pad and pencil were to be brought in from the outside.

Many similar rooms were opened later throughout the country. Our files give evidence of more than thirty colleges that came to us for suggestions, perhaps the most elaborate room being built at the University of Minnesota.

The best part of the Farnsworth were the fine young men who read there. No end of stories could be told of experiences with students, the attitude of individuals and the appreciation of the pleasure they have received. The habitual readers soon acquired a sense of possession. Early I noticed that they did not ask if such or such a book were there, but "Have we such or such a book?" I liked the "we."

A few outstanding incidents come to mind that may illustrate some of the aspects of life in this room. A freshman stood half-dazed one day before the Temptation Shelves. These were books selected for their power to awaken and hold interest. When I offered the evidently needed help his answer was somewhat startling. "Say, I never read a book through in my life. Do you think I could find something I could stick at?"

Here was a call for quick action. It demanded taking the measure of the man and running over in my mind the possibilities of making him a permanent reader. Evidently he was from a small town and from a home probably with no whatnot of books even. He was young for his years and did not look like one yet much interested in girls. It must be a real man's book, interesting enough to hold his attention, short enough not to be discouraging, but long enough to qualify as a book, not merely a short story.

In less time than it takes to write this, I handed him Conrad's *Typhoon*. He never left his chair until he turned the last page.

From that day he became a constant reader. Within six months he was asking me if I had read such and such a book. When he asked if I knew an author named Louisa Alcott and had I read *Little Women* I knew he was exploring the magic land of literature with the addition of the feminine interest.

One morning when he was near the end of his senior year as indicated by the gown he was wearing, with tasseled cap lying on the window, he was reading as usual. I was interested to see that he was again reading *Typhoon*.

"You see," he said, "I'm reading it again. I liked it when you gave it to me before but now I see so much in it that I didn't appreciate then — characterization, philosophy, and marvelous description. I shall always think of you when I see this book."

When he left college, it was to become a teacher of English in one of the good Massachusetts high schools. He later became a superintendent of schools in another state.

Rarely was there any occasion to say anything about behavior, although now and then a gentle reminder was necessary. A young man one day asked for something by Jeffery Farnol. I handed him *The Broad Highway* and *The Amateur Gentleman*. He chose the first and settled himself in one of the big brown leather chairs by the window, lolling lazily with both feet extended to the limit of their tether and heels grinding into the seat of a delicate rush-bottomed chair.

I approached, looking eloquently at the offending shoes, but without effect.

"You evidently took the wrong book," I remarked, "You should have taken *The Amateur Gentleman*.

The remark penetrated and the feet found their proper level.

Every spring there was the mad hunt for positions. The possibilities and the discouragements in finding and deciding on the "right" one needed to be talked over with someone, and many came to me for that purpose. Is it better to take a position in a great establishment, unimportant but with possibilities? Is it good sense to go to China with a certain oil company? Should a man take a position in a small private school or go into public school work? Of course none of these questions could be solved by me. All I could do was to help them see advantages and disadvantages, in fact, turn myself into a mental punching bag.

But the search was not always for the intellectual. I watched a man as he paused uncertainly in the vicinity of Emerson and Fielding. He looked as though he needed help, so I asked if he were looking for anything in particular.

"Yes," he answered with a smile, "I was looking to see if there was anyone here whom I could ask to change a dime for two nickels. I want to telephone."

Finding that I could be more helpful than Emerson or Fielding, I gave him the two nickels.

An attractive freshman appeared one day with three invitations to formal affairs in Boston. One could see that he was accustomed to attending such events, but Boston was new to him and he had all the horror of the young in making a social error. He wanted to know when, on what sort of stationery, and in what form he should offer his acceptance to meet the approval of Boston. I did the best I could for him although I was no authority in the matter.

In any group of students there is bound to be embryonic evidence of writing ability. Men out for places on the *Crimson* or other college publications came for news items or suggestions for editorials. Poetry is much in vogue with youth, and pages of manuscripts came under my eye each year. Romances, short stories, plays, and even novels came shyly for criticism when the writer could not quite muster his courage to approach an instructor. If ever I was any help it was in getting the prospective author to formulate his own ideas and by talking them out, discover things that he might not have brought to light by pondering them alone. Some went far enough to submit their articles to editors. Then rejection slips and the unsuccessful manuscripts came with the author for consolation or enouragement. Over an occasional acceptance there was great rejoicing.

This all tended to keep me in touch with young life and its eager and tremendous force. Without the spirit of youth the world would soon be dead. Let them rush headlong, sometimes in the wrong direction, but let us be grateful that they have the energy and enthusiasm thus to furnish the motive power for the world. Older people have their value at the steering wheel, but the driving force is youth.

In early April, 1917, I went to New York for a few days. Everything was running smoothly and life was as normal as it had been since Europe had become involved in the Great War. It was during these days that America made its decision to join the Allies. I returned to a changed Harvard. Books had been thrown aside and Harvard had stampeded to enlist.

The dormitories had been turned into barracks, with barrack simplicity — bed, chair, table. There were no facilities for study. Students marched in military formation into the library, which became one great study hall, with never room enough, even when the marble stairs were utilized, as they often were even to capacity. The Farnsworth Room no longer was a place for leisure reading, but each evening saw each chair occupied.

In some way it became known that I had been a teacher and knew trigonometry, which was required of all those in navy training. The news spread until one after another came to me for help. Although I was not due in the library in the evening, I made it a habit to be there, for with conditions as they were, so far from normal, it seemed best to know personally what was going on. The trigonometry made an excellent reason, for there was sure to be some student who would welcome me gladly. Often I made special appointments with such as needed some extra boosting.

After the war, several changes were needed in the location of libraries. The original freshman dormitories were remote from the Yard. Professor Chester N. Greenough was responsible for the idea of making rooms in McKinlock Hall into a library cosily accessible to freshmen. One room was given over to history and the other to a room similar in purpose to the Farnsworth Room, but modified to the different conditions, especially to the lifting of the ban on study. On the evening of its opening, Mrs. Lowell sent over a box of ashes from her own fireplace for the foundation of the first fire in the new library.

This library was moved from pillar to post until it was combined with the fine library at the Harvard Union, and I was asked to take charge of this reorganization. Even house libraries were also organized in Eliot, Adams, Dunstan, Kirkland, Leveritt, Lowell, and Winthrop, and I had the privilege of selecting books and supervising them under the general direction of the director, Robert P. Blake.

In 1923 Harvard was notified that Amy Lowell had designated in her will that Harvard was to have the pick of her library. The letter asked that the college appoint a committee, which with an expert, Mr. Goodspeed, appointed by Mrs. Russell for the Estate, would make the selections. Mr. Lane assigned Miss Tucker and me to this responsibility.

Miss Lowell, even before she became well known as a poet and lecturer, had the reputation for being a wise and discriminating buyer of rare books. I had heard much of her and her purchases through Luther and had read all I could about her collection, so it was another great dream fulfilled to be invited to browse among her books and help in the selection.

The world rarely is more beautiful than it was that first day that we turned into Sevenels, stepping immediately into the seclusion and the blazing glory which is New England's on the first of June. A gravel driveway wound under spreading and venerable trees and past blossoming shrubs — pink weigela, rose-red rhododendrons, and clumps of columbine. What a delight, too, to discover a lilac bush, purple with belated bloom — lilacs of Miss Lowell's exquisite poem. And so, loitering along, with beauty at every turn, we came to the great house and to the library.

This was a vast room, walled with bookcases. Books filled every available space of the house, from the third story down to the beautiful library. Books were everywhere, in every room, in halls, in passageways, on the floor, on every desk and table, threatening, as Miss Lowell herself once said, to crowd her out of house and home.

This is no place to go into detail over the collection and selection. They have been enumerated in many places. Our first concern was with first editions and associational copies and of these were great numbers. Personally, I found a solemn delight in handling the whole set of her Rollo books, which she had written about so happily and which she loved as I loved my Lucy books.

Kipling, Yeats, and Carroll

F lora had for many years been gathering together the printed and manuscript material by and relating to Rudyard Kipling. One summer she was to have the opportunity of consulting with several authorities in London, hoping to finish the bibliography that Luther had begun before his death. Now after much correspondence with A.S. Watt, Kipling's literary agent, and with the lawyer, they had asked to see the manuscript. Accordingly her plans were made for a summer in England, and I made plans to go with her.

Can one ever forget the excitement of that first glimpse of England's shores? I have since made many crossings, but each time I experience a deep emotional joy at the sight of and the actual landing on the land that is England.

We were among the first to disembark and took a very comfortable motor salon to Garland's, which in later years became one of our favorite "homes" in London.

Soon after settling ourselves, we made an appointment to see Mr. Watts and Mr. Kipling's lawyer, who went over Flora's manuscript. They approved of what she had done, and made many contacts possible for us that made possible an increase of the Kipling collection she already had and of items of interest to the Harvard Library.

A few days later an invitation came from Mrs. Kipling to visit her in her home, Bateman's, and to have tea with her. This was a great surprise and a pleasure we had not expected, for we knew that Mr. Kipling was just recovering from a serious illness and would not be able to see us himself.

We went to the Kiplings by way of Battle, stopping overnight at the old George Inn. It was a quaint old hotel with old silver, brass, and historical furniture of great interest. The next day (August 7, 1923), with a native at the wheel, we drove the twelve miles to Bateman's. When Flora told the driver that we wished to go to the Kiplings' home, his confusion showed that he had no idea what she was talking about. Flora had dwelt so long in the world of Kipling that she thought the direction adequate if given from any part of the world, for to her all roads led to Kipling.

"Mr. Rudyard Kipling, at Bateman's," she added with no effect.

"It's near Burwash." That penetrated and at Burwash we obtained definite directions.

As we rolled down the last hill we both recognized the house from its characteristic row of six chimneys. It was an old Elizabethan house of blue-gray stone, overgrown with roses and vines. The stone porch carried the date 1634, roughly hewn, but the house was actually built fourteen years earlier, according to Sussex records. The porch suggested the porch of a church or cloister, but it really was a symbol of prosperity. When a tradesman in those days began as a gentleman, he "set up the equivalent of a motor" by adding a porch to his habitation. Bateman's was built by such a tradesman and here was his porch of ceremony.

Passing between the high stone posts that finished the perfectly trimmed yew hedge, we took the few steps to the door. As the maid opened the door to us and ushered us through the halls to a room at the front, we could see that while the interior had been modernized to living comfort, it had been done in harmony with its historic character. It had been done so well that, although we sat some minutes in the charming room waiting for Mrs. Kipling, it is impossible to remember the room in detail. There was a great fireplace flanked by windows looking gardenward, comfortable chairs, and a table by a window giving upon the road screened by the high hedge. On the table was a great silver bowl inscribed with names of the great, filled with goldenrod just coming into bloom. Goldenrod does not grow in England at every roadside but has to be cultivated painstakingly.

The arrival of Mrs. Kipling put all thought of everything but the little lady out of mind. One thinks of her as little, for she is short. She came in, evidently from the garden, and was wearing a felt hat of blue that brought out the marvelous blue of her eyes. They and the charm of her manner eclipsed all else. Hers was an easy grace equal to any occasion from the meeting of royalty on even terms to the receiving so graciously of American callers in whom she could not have more than a passing interest.

For perhaps an hour we chatted about all sorts of things — the daughter's experience in taking people to Westminster and her saying when she came home: "I never before realized that the Abbey was anything but a place for important functions. I must get acquainted with it."

We talked about Rye and Battle, and Mrs. Kipling told us that we must not fail to see the beautiful old church at Battle. We saw it the next day and found it all she had claimed for it.

The entrance of the maid caused Mrs. Kipling to rise and usher us into the quaint dining hall. Above were the great rafters dark with age, as was the refectory table showing such a patina as only time can give and now holding the modern tea.

Mrs. Kipling took her place in a highback carved chair at the end of the table. Flora and I were placed on opposite sides on old monastic benches that ran the short length on the two sides of the table. The tea service was on a large round silver tray with hammered rim wide enough to take the smaller pieces of the service and the cups and saucers. The teakettle was plain and very handsome. With the tea we had thin bread and butter without which no English tea is complete, hot buttered scones, two kinds of cake and a square cookielike affair whose composition we were asked to guess. It was an oatmeal cake but very dressed up. With it all was a medlar jelly which Mrs. Kipling explained came from a tree in their garden and was similar to a quince.

After the tea came the glory of a tour of the surrounding gardens. From the side door we stepped out upon such turf as only England, and I suspect only Sussex, can produce. We followed the stone path down past lily pool and rose garden. When the wheel of the old mill was replaced by turbines to furnish electricity, the grindstones were broken up and laid for these walks. Following their irregular outlines the gray-green thyme grows so tight to the stones that it looks as though the color had been laid on with a brush.

We followed the walk along a row of blossoming lavender, its dusty looking foliage contrasting with the tall spikes of fragrant bloom, a bunch of which Mrs. Kipling gathered for each of us.

Back of the lavender rose a wall of yellow blossoms, while in front and close to the walk, was a side border of old-fashioned pinks. The cultivated garden gradually wandered off into the wild until we came to the "Friendly Brook" and the medlar tree.

We did not go as far as "Pook's Hill" but returned by way of the kitchen garden, the servant's quarters, and rows and rows of yew trees. She showed us how she was trying to train the Japanese yew to grow in such a way as to leave square windows through which one could catch a glimpse of the hills beyond but which would also ensure privacy. Flowers were tucked in between the vegetables. A few sunflowers in the corner, marigolds and asters at the ends of the bean rows, zinneas here and there, and other domestic flowers had settled down everywhere without interfering with the vegetables and making a useful garden a thing of beauty.

Courtesy of the National Trust and David Sellman.

The gardens at Bateman's

Back of the house were the old cast houses where in the olden days much good brewing was done. Now the houses with their exterior unchanged have been converted into comfortable rooms as a necessary annex to the main house.

Wandering back to the front of the house, our man was summoned — he had had his comfortable tea — and we drove away after a grateful "goodbye" and many a backward glance at what to Flora was almost a shrine and to me the scene of a delightful afternoon ever after to be woven into all my reading of Kipling.

Several years later when we were again in London, we received another invitation to Bateman's, this time from both Mr. and Mrs. Kipling. The bibliography had been published with full approval after much correspondence between Flora and the Kiplings, and now we were to have the pleasure of meeting him for the first time.

The day for our visit was typically English, rain and sunshine alternating. Sheep in the fields were picturesque, fields of grain divided by dark hedges, hay cut and "drying" hopefully in spite of weather, the sun bursting through at intervals and then without warning the patter of a quick shower. We had a good chauffeur for this trip and the car was a beautiful one, upholstered in blue leather and well appointed so the trip from Rye to Bateman's was delightful in spite of the weather.

This time as the maid opened the door, we were greeted by the frantic barking of two black Aberdeen terriers, who stopped immediately at the sound of the master's command. Mr. Kipling greeted us cordially. He looked exactly as I had expected only he wore a much pleasanter expression than is sometimes attributed to him. His eyebrows were darker and shaggier than I had pictured, but he made us feel most welcome. Mrs. Kipling was very thin and showed traces of her severe illness in Bermuda but said that she was gaining steadily.

For tea, we sat as before at the handsome old oak table. The dogs were a recognized part of the tea party. In addition to the usual English thin sandwiches and small cakes, there was a round cake frosted in two layers and red raspberries and cream. Before beginning tea, Mr. Kipling fed the dogs bisquit from their own plates which stood on his right. The dogs' names were James and Wampho — as nearly as I can remember the spelling.

After the tea and much interesting conversation, Mr. Kipling said, "Do you suppose they will go the rounds?" This was a trick that hadn't been used in many months. He put small biscuit bits on five chairs around the room and then called the dogs to "go the rounds," which they did with little prompting.

We later made a garden tour as before. Judy, not a pure bred dog as the others were, tried to join us but the two aristocrats would have none of her. "James and Wampho are confirmed bachelors," Mr. Kipling remarked. We passed on through the flower-lined paths to the swimming pool and tennis court abandoned since their daughter's marriage. The stream seemed so tiny as it ran along between deep banks but we were told that it sometimes invaded the entire garden even covering the tennis court. The lavender was as beautiful as we had remembered as were the garden pinks and deep red colve carnations.

As we reached the house again, Mrs. Kipling said, "Now let's have a fire and visit." Just then there was a mad commotion with the dogs down by the hedge. "Probably a rabbit" was Mr. Kipling's suggestion. Just then the creature came in sight, a graceful little hare fleeing over the ground with Wampho in hot pursuit. We watched until the hare was out of sight and then went to the house and the building of the fire, which Mr. Kipling did himself.

The talk now was upon books, the bibliography, translations of the Kipling stories, pirated editions, and many phases of his work. He showed us some of his treasures in oriental and classic books. He had a beautiful copy of the Koran from the Heath collection, which Mr. Heath had given to Mr. Kipling shortly before his death. There was a beautifully printed Latin book with initials in color, the blue being made from ground lapis lazuli. There was also a very interesting chain that had been made by a sea captain, complete in every detail to one described by Mr. Kipling in one of the *Just So* stories.

Wampho came in covered with burrs and grass seed —a weary looking dog he was, but James had not returned. Mr. Kipling was exceedingly worried, and after pacing for a minute or two, he turned to me and said, "Come to the gate with me, will you. I must find him." He was very excited and, blowing his whistle and calling, we traversed the fields and meadows in our search for the dog. Finally, discouraged, we returned to the house and found James sitting quietly just under the step.

"You may think me silly," Mr. Kipling remarked as he sank into a chair, "But since our daughter went away, the dogs are all we have left."

It was very touching.

As we left the house Mr. Kipling put us into the car.

"Where did you find such a car," he asked.

"Rye."

"Cars are improving in Rye. That's a nice one."

Then he closed the door and both waved their good-byes as the car started.

Flora and I made a short trip to London one November. We both had work involving much time in the library of the British Museum and several appointments to keep. Flora was working on Henry James and I was searching for copies of and about Herman Melville that were lacking in our Harvard collection. Flora had finished editing the letters of Charles Dickens to Charles Lever. Hyder Rollins, Professor of English at Harvard, had written the introduction. He was a good friend of ours, who lived close to us in Cambridge and who often had Thanksgiving dinner with us. We had several pleasant visits with him at this time when we were all in London. He had written several important works on Keats, Shakespeare, and Pepys so it was always interesting to be with him. One evening he invited us to dinner and to see John Galsworthy's play "Old English" at the Theatre Royal which we found delightful.

The real highlight of this trip, however, we owe mainly to the exceedingly heavy fog which enveloped London that year. We were studying in a quaint old hotel which was long a favorite resort of literary and artistic people. Here Whistler and Henry James used to come, and it was the home of Sir Rider Haggard when business called him to the city. This was where Professor Brested stayed on his return from the opening of the tomb of Tutankh-amen and went forth for his audience with King George.

Here we had the delight of several days' association with Mr. and Mrs. William Butler Yeats — thanks to the fog. A three-day fog had shut down completely on the great city. Looking down Suffolk Street, toward Pall Mall, nothing was visible but an occasional struggling light showing but as a feeble flame of a candle through the smothering fog. At all strategic points, flames flared and blazed warningly to the few buses that still courageously threaded Whitehall, Charing Cross, and Trafalgar. But within it was comfortable and a coal fire was glowing in the grate.

Mr. and Mrs. Yeats, a much-traveled Englishman, Flora, and I settled down for our coffee and cigarettes and a pleasant visit.

No picture of Mr. Yeats can do him justice, for there is a fresh coloring of his clear skin and the quiet serenity of his eyes. There is a great charm in the calmness of his face in repose.

We talked about contemporary American and English writers and this brought forth many surprises. Edwin Arlington Robinson was at that time accorded almost first rank among American poets, but Mr. Yeats had not heard of him. He thought that Amy Lowell had no great following in England in spite of Clement Shorter's great admiration for her and her work. He knew and admired Robert Frost and recognized the poetic value of Edgar Lee Masters' *Spoon River Anthology*. He admitted that poets didn't know much about other poets. He had high praise for Robert Bridges and he and Ezra Pound were close personal friends.

Of his own work he spoke with modest frankness. When I told him I had known him first through "Heart's Desire" and that I had been deeply moved by seeing "The Hour Glass" acted by some young people, he smiled and said, "A renegade Catholic once told me that seeing that little play had restored him to the fold of the church."

His discussion of the political conditions in Ireland was a revelation to us. He had had an active part in the establishment of the Irish Free State, and was still carrying grave responsibilities. Belonging as he did to the Protestant minority his every word was surprisingly free of any trace of prejudice. The love for Ireland was deep in his heart and for that and that alone he worked.

Would that I could produce the charm of his gentle speech and the sympathetic tenderness of his attitude toward his countrymen, whether Protestant or Roman Catholic. His rich Irish laugh will never be forgotten as he told us interesting stories or enjoyed the flavor of clever repartee.

Several trips to London were spent in collecting data for a bibliography of Lewis Carroll's work and for an edition of *The Rectory Umbrella* and *Misch-Masch*. Mr. Falconer Madan of the Bodleian was very helpful. He obtained permission for me to see Lewis Carroll's rooms and all associated and available material. He brought out three file boxes and several books for me to see. I needed to know what was lacking in our collection at Harvard. He called my attention to the running numbers which

Carroll put on all his letters and similar communications and how with a little practice one could date things accordingly.

I also had the cooperation of Mr. Sidney Hodgson, a rare book dealer in Chancery Lane and of Spencer's on New Oxford Street, where I found much good material, including a list of Lewis Carroll's friends.

One summer I received an invitation from Major C.H.W. Dodgson, Lewis Carroll's nephew and the one responsible for the estate, to visit him and his sisters at their home in Guilford. I followed the directions and got off at the London Road Station and found Luss Cottage easily. Just as I opened the gate, a young lady came out of the house and greeted me most cordially. She took me into the quite typical English small drawing room where her sister, Miss Manella, was equally cordial.

They offered me coffee or wine and we had a very profitable visit about their famous uncle, at the end of which they told me that Major Dodgson, who had been detained in the city, had given his assurances that permission would be sent to me in writing for the editions I planned.

I later had several visits with Major Dodgson, including tea at Dodgson Cottage, London Road, where I saw the *Rectory Umbrella* and *Alice* in Dutch and also some mathematics papers. After tea I called on Charles L. Dodgson's only surviving sister, who was ninety years old.

I thought the hardest part of my search was over; I had an American publisher, I had succeeded in getting permission of the heirs, I had found an English publisher who did publish the editions. However, by that time, the Depression had come and the American publishers did not dare venture upon the project, so the book never had much circulation in this country.

Retirement

As the days of my retirement drew near, the pictures of Boston and Cambridge and of Harvard Yard grew even more persistently cherished.

I never could cross Harvard Bridge going to or from Cambridge without experiencing a new thrill of pleasure in the scene before me. It was never the same. At night the scene was like a jewel rimmed by the encircling lights; by day it was tree-bordered. On the Boston side the Esplanade, a gray and green ribbon, ran from bridge to bridge, and back of it rose in solid phalanx the dignified old houses of Beacon Street. There is no other red like that of the rich-hued, time- mellowed tone of old brick. Above the green of the Esplanade, I delighted in the spires and towers as they lifted against the sky and seemed to climb Beacon Hill toward the golden dome of the State House glittering in the sunlight, or gleaming through the dusk.

On the Cambridge side stood the long symmetrical stretch of the Institute of Technology buildings, pleasing in proportion and line, while the dome of the library, like the Pantheon, "stands in calm and serene beauty," crowning it all.

In going from Cambridge to Boston, I often played a fascinating game. Between the spire of the New Old South Church and the Custom House tower, there were, the first time I thought to count them, just seven pinnacles of varying height. Never afterwards was I able to make the number come out exactly seven. Sometimes the count ran to nine or ten, to my confusion; often it fell short of the original seven. The car always rumbled off the bridge before I could be completely satisfied.

When the river was ice-locked, cloud-hung and snow-walled in glittering cold, it would inspire the brush of a Rockwell Kent. The gulls occasionally ventured up as far as the lower side of the bridge, where they would sit on the floating ice, fluffy balls of white. There seemed to be one strange thing about these gulls; I never caught them in flight. Either they were there, immovable as sphinxes, or they were not there.

There is no end of the pictures. On pleasant days the Esplanade was warm with human interest. Regardless of weather, however, the Harvard shells, youth propelled, would shoot arrow-straight up the river and disappear around the bend. Launches fussed around the Basin. When storm clouds gathered in the west, lightning quickly changed the scene. When the fog crept in from the sea, there was no river at all.

I loved to look out from the Farnsworth Room toward the new and beautiful Memorial Chapel facing Widener. I couldn't help contrasting the intervening space and the quadrangle with the famous Tom Quad at Oxford. There was not much difference in size but a vast difference in the ways of the students. Tom Quad, as I remembered it, was one broad expanse of lawn with such sod as only centuries can produce. This expanse is cut by two walks intersecting at right angles in the center, where a fountain plays. Not another path crosses the green. I doubt if a Christ Church man ever steps off the surrounding terrace and walk except upon the intersecting walks and those crossing at right angles.

Widener Quadrangle, on the contrary, is traversed by a maze of walks going in every direction that a student could wish to go. I remember a time when only two or three walks crossed this space, but year after year they have increased in number. It is the habit of the American youth to go in a bee line to his objective. Why should he turn square corners when he sees a short cut with no obstruction except the invisible one of possibly marring the grass? When several go habitually in the same direction it does not take long to wear a clearly defined path. When this is accomplished then the authorities see that a macadam path makes the shadow permanent.

These crowds that surged over these paths at the close of every hour seemed a curious crowd. Rarely did I see two students walking together. Each one seemed to be going his

Memorial Chapel

own way bent on his own thoughts and business.

When I first watched these men from my window, most were carrying bulging Boston bags. These bags always seemed to me to be the ugliest of carriers. They were always packed to overflowing, contents straining against the strap which never could quite hold the contents together. Those have almost entirely disappeared. Then was the vogue for the green bag and one or two were still in evidence. They were especially popular with law students, for they seemed best able to sustain the weight of the law, especially when the string was replaced by a strong strap. The briefcase has held its own share of popularity for some time now.

I used to enjoy the glimpses I frequently had of President Lowell, with Phantom running ahead or scampering to keep up. When Phantom was along one knew that the president was enjoying a brief respite from heavy affairs of administration, because when duties were heavy, Phantom was not called into conference. It was a joy to see this admirable man come swinging up Widener's steps, two at a time, regardless of his seventy-fifth year.

On days when the rain came down in torrents these Harvard men trudged through it indifferently and umbrellaless. A man would have lost caste to be caught in Harvard Yard under an umbrella. Raincoats were the only concession to the weather and with these, the shabbier the better. Some colleges could make a scene of color even on a rainy day because of the bright-hued raincoats, but not Harvard. Their nearest concession was the yellow Cape Cod slicker or oilskin of the fisherman. One year almost nothing else was visible, but for that there was a reason. The Yale-Harvard game was played in a pouring rain and the traffic in the Stadium in slickers was tremendous. Boston was sold out and every enthusiastic rooter, having become the forced possessor of a slicker, made use of it throughout the year.

It seemed impossible in 1932 when President Lowell announced his retirement that anyone else could possibly occupy his place and I like to think no one really has. The waves pass over but the ripples and achievements of past leaders are not lost. The new President, James Bryant Conant, has in his turn brought his own unique and admirable qualities of leadership to the college and these too will never be lost.

A. Lawrence Lowell sets a fast pace.

Retirement was anticipated as a long looked-for time for writing — unbroken hours at the typewriter — watching the ideas jotted down in many notebooks throughout the busy years unfold into finished creations. But, as has been the experience of many before me, I have discovered that one does her best work when she is so busy that there doesn't seem to be any time for it. I have also found that since World War II requirements have changed radically, and although I have published numerous articles these past years, many more have found their way back. On writing many stories there is no end, but much returning is a weariness to the flesh.

My chief writing pleasure has been this story of an ordinary woman. I hope that it will encourage others to see life as a whole; that the accomplishments and loyalties of each hour and day bring in the end some satisfaction and sometimes unbelievable experiences.

I carry on a voluminous correspondence because my friends are scattered over the earth. I still hear from and have visits from many of my former students as they pass through Boston. Flowers and gifts from them overwhelm me with a deep sense of gratitude. On my ninetieth birthday I received one hundred and fifty personal notes and 90 American Beauty roses from my Grand Rapids "boys and girls" of fifty years ago. Each Christmas brings an equal number of notes and letters, including a check from my "elevator boy" in Grand Rapids who has not failed in over forty years. How can one be grateful enough for such friends?

Flora and I listen to every Harvard game by radio, and we feel that we can follow the game almost as well as we could in the stadium. In fact, we have such a good time and make so many comments on the plays that anyone hearing us might wonder why we were not employed by the coaching staff. I suppose it may seem strange that a woman of ninety-two could enjoy a football game as I do. I find baseball equally exciting and make up my own diagram of the field, the teams and the scoring.

I am somewhat handicapped but I can almost hear what people think, and my heart and spirits seem to keep reasonably young. My nurse Emma takes good care of me, and my friends come to see me bringing books, flowers, and food, and sharing ideas as well as a fashion show whenever a new dress is purchased.

As I lay in bed this morning after I had had my breakfast I decided that I would begin to keep a daily list of all the nice things that happen to me. I must think of a good name to call the list, but that should not be too difficult. There will be no difficulty in remembering the items to go into it, not forgetting the time, thoughts and love in all.

We have had as yet this fall only one flurry of snow, but we shall have plenty before long. Depend upon New England for that. It will not disturb me, however, for I shall keep under cover. Our apartment is always warm and I shall keep pretty close to my comfortable quarters. With windows on three sides, I get all the sun that shines and a glimpse of the outside world. Every night when I get into bed, I return thanks that I have so many blessings that I go to sleep before I can count them. Once I had two dear sisters. I now return thanks for the countless pleasant memories of Blanche, and the countless reminders of Maud, who is so much like our mother in her joyous ability to make any day a holiday. Every special day brings a ring at the door with some little remembrance from her in far-off Michigan. One Sunday morning in spring a lovely box of pansies arrived — purple and yellow faces assuring me that I was indeed being thought of — and that beauty was close at hand in spite of a snowy blizzard beating against the windows.

My niece Emma has just taken a bowl of her good soup up to Flora but did not get any response to her ring. Flora is a great sleeper and does not hear very well. Emma is watching me with a "supper is almost ready" look in her eye. Her little grandchild was in some days ago, and after looking me over she said, "She's not sick. She just sits in the big chair and laughs and talks just like anyone else."

From the *Harvard Alumni Bulletin,* October 14, 1950

The death of Mrs. Florence Cushman Milner on September 11 at the age of 95 calls to mind the days when this friendly and sympathetic lady was the proprietress of the Henry Weston Farnsworth Room, then located in Widener Library. Many were the receptive minds entrusted to her ministrations, for it was her pleasant duty to insure that this sanctuary was used only by those reading for pleasure, those discovering the wonders of library browsing for themselves. One of Mrs. Milner's boys was Thomas Wolfe, A.M. '22, whose memories of the Farnsworth Room were incorporated in early drafts of his novel *Of Time and the River.* The loneliness of Eugene Gant was tempered and soothed by the moments he spent under the friendly lamps of the Farnsworth Room and in the vast stacks of the library itself. This is the way some of the rejected passages read (text is from Richard S. Kennedy's "Thomas Wolfe at Harvard, 1920-1923," *Harvard Library Bulletin*, Autumn, 1950).

"There was a room (if it has gone the rest can perish) on the right hand of the entrance to Widener Library. It had lined in its reachable and encircling shelves, several thousand most noble books. It was furnished as well with spacious rump-receiving chairs and couches . . . .

"The light was mellow; the decoration quiet and soothing; the place was governed by a kindly ponderous woman of sixty years, who allowed the young men catholic liberty of their arms, legs, thighs; a man might read asprawl without complaint. To this room daily he came; before he left he had gutted the place of all he had not previously read . . . .

"And as, sunk in the deep luxury of the Farnsworth Room, he heard remotely the hideous clamour of the Cambridge street cars, the conviction grew in him. Almost all that the University had to offer him was in that room; in later years when his memories of the whole scene was phantasmal as painted smoke, the solid and permanent outlines of that room, the exact placing of the books on the shelves, all remained minutely fixed; that place was freedom heaven, Harvard — the one place he had found where utter freedom had been given to him, to think, say what he liked.

"And this, in the end was what Harvard came to mean to him: a room of fine books and spacious chairs. Few places have meant more."